# Spiritual Activism

·······

*Keys to Personal and Political Success*

WANDA KRAUSE

**TURNING
STONE
PRESS**

First published in 2013 by
Turning Stone Press, an imprint of
Red Wheel/Weiser, LLC
With offices at:
665 Third Street, Suite 400
San Francisco, CA 94107
*www.redwheelweiser.com*

Copyright © 2013 by Wanda Krause

ISBN: 978-1-61852-067-8

Cover design by Jim Warner
Cover image: Kochneva Tetyana/Shutterstock

Printed in the United States of America
10 9 8 7 6 5 4 3 2 1

*For my parents,*
*Pam Herdes and Werner Krause*

# Contents

# Acknowledgements

First I would like to thank all the spiritual activists who allowed me to interview them and expose their dreams and goals in this work. Sometimes I asked personal questions around motivation and the trials they endured. They all had the courage to go back and relive moments, allowing me to gain the deeper sense and power of experience. In this way I could grasp their choices to honor the purpose of their trials. I have so often walked away from meetings with these people truly flabbergasted at the expanse of their souls and the intensity of their wills. Yet, their notable feature was consistently humility in describing what they do. I hope I have conveyed how important their struggles are for all of us. Though, I will confirm, more personally, that I found myself reading their beautiful examples over and over towards the end of writing this book when one of my own dark nights of the soul hit. Their examples have carried me through and crucially provided the inspiration, spiritual learning, and faith I need too.

The ability to recognize the keys to success and the spiritual wisdoms has also been through a long journey of learning, starting well before formal study. Spiritual learning has been made possible through several souls. These firstly include my mother, who is religious, and my father, who shunned religion but finds his guidance through nature. Their principles and taking the family out into the wilderness for extended periods to appreciate and breathe All That Is has helped me embrace my own spirit and life direction. Of course, my parents are not perfect but because of that they have been ideal for the life lessons I have needed to grow. Thank you. I would never be the person I am without all you have done for me. A more expanded learning than mainstream academia has been through spiritual teachers who have given their time, authors I have never met, and many others, such as a few of the systems, integral, and political thinkers. My teachers include my children and wise friends.

Always having been my first reader, thanks to Jasser Auda for providing a critical eye and support. This endeavor may have never made it to print without all you've done. Thanks to Noreen Ayesha for believing in this work. Noreen, you are immensely appreciated for your coaching throughout the entire period of writing this book. Thanks to Maxwell Carey for his political insights and a few corrections. Thanks to my brothers for inspiring me to recognize lessons and choices that directly relate to the messages of this book. Thanks Daniel for critical feedback on the book. Finally, I extend my gratitude to the editorial team at Turning Stone Press for their diligence and for bringing this book to final form.

# Introduction

*". . . have the courage to follow your heart and intuition."*
—Steve Jobs

## 1

On February 24, 1955 a baby boy was born to Syrian father Abdulfattah studying in the U.S. and American mother Joanne of German descent living in rural Wisconsin. Both were 23 years old and not married. Not intending to elope at that time, Joanne had seriously considered and weighed her options before the birth. Given that she came from a small Wisconsin Catholic community, she ultimately decided against abortion and instead gave her baby boy up for adoption. The adoptive parents were both high school dropouts—Paul, a mechanic, and Clara, a bookkeeper.

Psychologists and sociologists still define early childhood experiences, such as supposedly being unwanted, or neglected, abused, or from poor or uneducated backgrounds, as the predictors for having little success in life. By comparison, those individuals who grow up in well-adjusted and at least reasonably well-to-do households and who are raised by educated parents have the greatest chances for success. This view is also expressed in situational analysis theory. It developed from the personality traits theory that became popular in the 1930s. The personality traits theory viewed a likelihood of success and leadership as predetermined from birth. Biology and context, though dominating thoughts on success, have little explanatory power.

The baby boy who was chosen and adopted by Paul and Clara Jobs, Steve Jobs, became one of the greatest examples of success at the turn of our century. Yet, he does not fit some basic criteria.

A new theory was popularized in the 1970s that pointed out examples of "self-made" individuals who were, for example, born into poor families and rose to riches. Fortunately, for many of us who were not born into the "right" context or "right" biology, we are given examples of those who could still make it—despite agency or affiliation. At least we glimpse the fact that the door isn't shut. Yet, such a broad sweeping claim does not explain why or how these particular individuals rose to success beyond the mantra of hard work.

Hard work and discipline are important. But, sometimes, programs produce and uphold systems in which the hardest working people enable a certain order whereby those higher up in the power hierarchy derive benefits and well, then, don't need to work as hard. But the kind of hard work that has often been praised and subsumed under the American Dream is not going to help you achieve true success. According to the Economic Policy Institute, income growth for the top 1 percent of all U.S. income earners between 1979 and 2007 was 390 percent while, during that same time, the bottom 90 percent, only saw an increase of 5 percent.[1]

That same gap is also expanding, on a grander scale, between rich and poor countries. All the while, statistics indicate that lower and middle class individuals are working harder than ever. People who achieve the highest forms of success do it differently.

Steve Jobs, co-founder, chairman, and CEO of Apple Inc., who oversaw the development of iMac, iTunes, iPod, and iPad, is widely known as the charismatic pioneer of the personal computer revolution. He received a number of honors for his influence in the technology and music industries and conferred many titles, such as the "master evangelist of the digital age."[2] As evident by Jobs' accolades, despite his humble beginnings, psychologists, sociologists, and others miss the mark in identifying what enables leaders to emerge or have the right ingredients for success.

There is a piece to the puzzle that most experts are not getting. None of the traditional approaches can offer any meaningful analysis of Jobs' (or those like him) ascension. So, you cannot walk away with any useful insights for your path to success. More significantly, such thinking does not help in explaining what "success" really is. And how can you explain how to reach success if you do not know success as anything but fame, riches, or being recognized as a leader? Successful leader in what? The whole history of these theories of what makes a leader grew with the analysis of Hitler. So, what insight can any of us gain from hindsight?

## 2

There are umpteen attempts to understand what made people like Jobs successful. On October 5, 2012, marking the one year anniversary of Jobs' death after his battle with cancer, Fox News published an opinion editorial called "How to be a Success Like Steve Jobs." The publication hones in on "focus." Surely, you don't need to attend university or read anyone else's opinion to reach this conclusion.

Think about those of us who graduate with honors and straight As. Take the five of those who are closest to you and pinpoint where they are today. They are probably doing okay in a good, stable job. Now, think of those of us who were more creative, insightful, and active in pursuing other interests, regardless of academic achievement. Take the average of them, and I bet these have a more creative edge to the work they chose, have a less stable job, but in all aspects are doing better in life. Rational, objective logic as the thinking that we have come to value to define the successful is most certainly not what truly differentiates greatness and goodness from okayness or less. And guess what, Jobs got the idea early on. He dropped out of university to study what he was passionate about.

What so many of my interviewees have taught me is that when they need to get ahead, often desperately or passionately so, logic, even rational calculation, is never what they consider. It is not remotely first on the table. In other words, to have impact and really transform things means using something more than rational weighing, gathering opinion, expert consultation or resources. Our standard track for education isn't it. The high IQ some of us possess isn't it either. Don't misunderstand; rationality is not out the window for these people. The intelligence we measure for an IQ test is not irrelevant. These simply are not the first tools truly successful people use!

# 3

There is a simple fact that proves your ability to be successful and leave your footprint before you leave your physical body. You are here. Because you are here you have a purpose or, more accurately, purposes. To find and live your purposes is the first of all the keys to success. Fortunately, most of us have many challenges in life. These form the opportunity for life lessons. Lessons guide us to our purposes. These obstacles, hardships, and failures are no accident. These serve as guiding posts for our purpose. Some can be utterly painful. Yet, they are still gifts to push you to succeed at embracing your purpose, finding a higher consciousness, and living authentically.

To be alive is the biggest blessing. But the vast majority of people do not consciously know how to succeed with this blessing. It's similar to winning the lottery. Most people do not know how to use their sudden enormous wealth wisely and, consequently, go out and blow it. Statistics show interesting insights into those people who play the lottery. The vast majority of those who actually hit the jackpot lose much of it quickly. Not all, but most of those end up blowing it on useless items, end up with family squabbles over it, and wind up unhappy and unfulfilled. The rate of ensuing depression is marked. More sadly, whether with an obsession with winning the lottery, gambling or other empty imagined fixes, most such people never gained the skills to prosper. There are no quick fixes in life—well, aside from under very specific terms, which you will learn about in one of the case studies that illustrate exception to this universal law. Without understanding the wealth life offers and how to invest it, success will continue to elude you. Success is living your life purposes fully.

I have either researched or had the opportunity to observe the participation of hundreds of activists in various initiatives, philanthropic endeavors, and organizations from South America, North America, Europe, the Balkans, North Africa, the Arab Gulf, Southeast Asia, and East Asia intensively for over twelve years. There are various strategies for success and strategies for misery. Wherever you go, however, the guiding universal laws and principles for succeeding at life reign. I seek to deliver what I have gathered through studying, observing, and interviewing those individuals.

I cannot escape addressing a few glaring observations about the hundreds of activists that I have studied in relation to others. Individuals who grew up in well-adjusted homes with parents who pushed for an appreciation of education often have reasonable success in life. Some are extremely ambitious. However, they often have to work a lot harder to find the keys to live truly successfully—that is, with a sense of purpose and fulfillment. Perhaps life has not squeezed, or tested, these people enough.

On the other hand, those who have difficult childhoods or more than average challenges later on seem to have elected to learn a lot more in life. These range from personal trauma to experiencing the effects of war. The more you learn the more potential you have. And what you seek is what you will find. Some of these people were also pushed hard to appreciate a good education. What's more, nearly all of these people have been squeezed by life to an extent that they have been forced to learn the meaning of existence.

So, this is my conclusion about these individuals: they have, for one, greater chances to experience higher levels of success; and two, after learning the ropes gain greater opportunities to lead others to success. They often see more clearly the mess we are creating for ourselves. Ones who sought to affirm a core sense of selfhood and larger meaning from personal chaos recognize the greater oneness and chaos the world is in. They find purpose in doing something about this larger chaos.

I will remind you that the context of life lessons merely gives you a platform to succeed. It does not do it automatically for you. They are by no means any guarantee that you will lead and experience success or guide others to greater self-awareness and consciousness. People who succeed use life itself and the laws that govern life to experience the greatness and goodness life offers them. Life was never meant to be all uphill and happy. Yet, we have essential spiritual keys that can make the journey much more joyous, peaceful, and satisfying—that is, consciously meaningful and purposeful.

Another glaring observation: Most people I assess as powerful and advanced souls are very, very tough people. These are people whose family members will tell you— probably on your first meeting with them—that they are living with an incredibly strong personality. There is a resilience that is beyond rationality. But the difference between toughies and those who really create change for the good is that the latter are tough but soft. They like to see the good in people. Actually, they are more often downright naïve. No matter what they have seen, and probably because of what they have seen, they have chosen to grow in strength and compassion. These are the types of people who are truly successful—at life.

I have learned that these people are built and molded through their responses to life's trials. They don't just appear out of nowhere. How the successful person responds is highly dependent upon an ability to recognize and use the right keys to learn and grow from life's experiences.

**4**

In an interview on *60 Minutes Overtime*, Bill Gates was asked to assess what made Jobs successful. Gates—who also dropped out of university—who, again in 2013, is the richest man on earth after giving away most of his wealth, answered: "He had an intuitive sense for marketing that was amazing." He pinpointed what he valued as essential. Jobs had confirmed his source for deeper knowledge and his drive to seek something larger than himself. Reflecting on his early search for the meaning of life and influences on his life direction, he told his biographer, Walter Isaacson, "I began to realize that an intuitive understanding and consciousness was more significant than abstract thinking and intellectual logical analysis."[3]

He and others like him that I have observed or studied around the globe teach us about a higher or inner knowledge and about the use of spiritual keys for success. These keys work because they are linked to universal laws that govern our universe regardless of whether we choose to learn and live by them or not. Our actions all have consequences. People who choose to recognize the consequence of success use keys governed by basic physics. They consciously choose actions according to notions of principles. I call all such people who have learned these keys or principles and actively use them *spiritual activists*. They move beyond the material to embrace a higher intelligence—*and* experience real success.

A few clarifications are necessary. Some of those I have studied do not feel that they are spiritual at all. Some activists do not wish to be elevated to any notion of greatness as they assure me they have their share of past mistakes. Not everyone who I refer to as a spiritual activist affirms a religious belief. It should be noted that not all "religious" persons are actually spiritual or activists.

Recognizing those I have studied as *spiritual* in the way they pursue their dreams in no way is an attempt to confer holiness or religious devotion. And, of course, they are not perfect. But knowing they are imperfect, embracing that and growing from all their imperfect choices and circumstances is yet the point. The truly successful align their goals with conscious duty and purpose. Purpose is found in discovering why you are here and what you need to do. In all the case studies presented here, activists reflect something beyond rational opportunist thinking—a guidance, higher knowing, strong inner calling and principled action.

So, then what makes people unsuccessful? We interpret our life circumstances as bad. We cover up our uniqueness to fit in. We are taught to fill a void created by this madness with things that are not real. Sadly, we are led to overvalue the observable world of things—things around us. Those of us who do that devalue an inner core and when we do that we become fractured selves. In line with seeking progress, we were taught the only intelligence that matters is rationality. Even more unfortunate, we hide our feelings, emotions, religious or spiritual beliefs, our inner knowing, our inner guidance, our spontaneous creativity. This predicament is the recipe for "unsuccess."

Jobs did not devalue material gain, education, or logic. Rationality is not wrong. We need to use it. But it is simply not the highest form of intelligence. We need a higher form of thinking to get ourselves out of a mess we have created—and you will read of the many manifestations. Material things are not wrong, and they will fall into place, but they lead us away from what is real when we cannot recognize that they distract from what is.

My heart's desire and passion has been to learn how to really succeed at transforming situations and creating change. In this process, I have tried, applied, and even began teaching the dominant approaches. But most approaches do not work with principles that embrace critical aspects, such as intuition or the soul. Nor do they appreciate the full spectrum of the mind, culture, or how strategy itself becomes politically created and manipulated. They are not based on any notion of a higher meaning aside from getting, taking, and having. They fail to recognize how life's unique lessons are most certainly there to guide us, train us, and ready us to do something remarkable. They can't help you succeed in our fast changing world.

*Spiritual Activism* offers the essential keys to success, with success defined as achieving all that is going to help you live with purpose. I do not claim to exhaust all the universe's keys and laws here or even remotely know them all. There are many, but the principles presented are those that I found to be common among successful activists that I have spent years studying. I found these to be common among all the world's major mystical teachings, whether activists were aware of them or not.

The pages that follow allow you to see success from a holistic integral approach. They reveal these essential keys and illustrate how truly successful people use them. The principles work for your personal growth, family, relationships, community, and the business and political arenas. All of these spheres are governed by the same laws and are interconnected. One key might be more critical than another in a given situation, or entirely appropriate for the business world but not relationships, for example.

Now, given what we know about the pursuit of success, the questions we ought to be asking are, what is *real* success? And, can I experience real success? You have to. The purpose of this book is to illustrate *how*. You will learn twelve keys to succeed. Because any issue you seek to address or any goal you seek to achieve is most assuredly embedded in power hierarchies, these keys are essential to change dynamics, not just solve problems or get you from point A to point B. You will meet individuals who illustrate what success truly is and how to experience it. It is your birthright and more—it is a responsibility to be successful. In this book, I am going to show you how to reclaim this birthright.

My interest in people succeeding at whatever greatness and goodness they want is in the ripple effect they must have on the world according to universal law. My wider vision is systemic change created by you fulfilling your heart's desire. The world is in desperate need of radical change, if more of us only knew. The keys and strategies offered are actually simple and follow an essential premise—living your purpose—as articulated below:

> Your time is limited so don't waste it living someone else's life. Don't be trapped by dogma—which is living with the results of other people's thinking. Don't let the noise of others' opinions drown out your inner voice. And most important, have the courage to follow your heart and intuition. They somehow know what you truly want to become. Everything else is secondary.
>
> —*Steve Jobs, Stanford Commencement Address*

~

～

# PART ONE

*Keys to Success*

～

$\backsim$ 1 $\backsim$

# Key #1: Living your Purpose

*Real success starts with discovering the reason you have your
unique life, with all its trials and circumstances—why you were
gifted with it, and what you need to do with it.*

## Introduction

According to the Merriam-Webster Dictionary, success is
1) the degree or measure of succeeding, and 2) the attainment of a favorable or desired outcome; also the attainment of wealth, favor or eminence.

But how do you define what is worthy of pursuit? Do
you really think you will wish you had accumulated more
to leave behind? You won't. A more prestigious position? Not likely. On your deathbed you will surely have
a different perspective about the life you just lived. You
will have a few moments in which you realize what was
most important. In fact, we all already know in our inner
knowing, our intuition, what is most important. But people who end up truly successful, at some point resolved to
choose listening to their own inner knowing. They will
see the reflections of success around them through the
eyes of loved ones and from within their hearts. You will
want to be one of those—not one of those who climbed

up to the end of the ladder only to discover they positioned it against the wrong wall. Real success starts with discovering the reason you have your unique life, with all its trials and circumstances—why you were gifted with it, and what you need to do with it.

The way we are pursuing success does not work because the experience of it does not last. More sadly, it serves largely to create a hole in our hearts that drives us to clamor at more to feel better. We simply wouldn't have ever increasing crime rates, broken homes, rates of suicide and depression, the gap between rich and poor and starving, civil wars and terror around the globe if the way we understood and pursued success entailed *real* success. Wealth, favor, and eminence? For what purpose?

Whenever I witness individuals reclaim their birthright to seek real success I experience joy. Especially if I believe I played any minute role, whatsoever, I have attained one of my measures of success. Each step I make in experiencing success lets me know I am on my own path to fulfilling my purpose. Success, I have learned, is not something, however, that you can always measure tangibly. As some of the activists will illustrate and I have learned through my own struggles, oftentimes the success comes from an inner measure of experience in the giving and planting, even when the harvest is delayed.

## A Few Reminders of My Life Path

It takes most of us years. Sadly, as a few accounts of wise last words from awakened individuals have imparted to us, it took too long to recognize the deeper meaning of success. Admittedly, it was not long ago that I was working extreme hours and feeling really bad about it.

In my position, I was nicely placed up the evolutionary ladder of my career. I complained to my older brother, Michael. "What is career anyway?" he said to me at the time. He pointed out, "Career isn't going to matter on your deathbed." Yes, for what was I drowning myself in long hours of work, power struggles, and the related stress while each family member needed me in ways I was not fully present to give?

In many ways such pursuits do give the promise of success and could be a part of it, but a true sense of attainment for me was utterly shallow. I was ignoring a truer sense of being and mixing ego with desire—and, then: bang. I ran into the proverbial brick wall. It was too much; unsustainable for any human, let alone anyone attached to a family. But here I was feeling torn, stretched, underappreciated, not so healthy, not so connected to loved ones and friends, and giving less to my spiritual practice.

For the first time in months, I was laying on the beach in the sun. I was watching my seven-year-old daughter on the water during her sailing lesson while I was holding a book called *Everyday Grace* by Marianne Williamson. After my brother's feedback I was waking up. And after another stressful and empty day I was really soaking up the seaside peace, laughter, and beauty, despite the heat of +40 degrees Celsius; yet, still unsure about taking a leap of change. Williamson's words drew me to the bigger picture. I flipped to the next page and read her quote to an opening chapter:

"You would rather be anywhere than going into this meeting. You think about being at the movies, being on the beach, being with your kids—being anywhere but here. The people waiting on the other side of that door don't know who you are or even seem to care. You don't have the feeling they really want you to succeed. You can't believe you work here. Welcome to your career. . . ."[4]

## Understanding Real Success

I want to draw attention to a few things exposed through my own personal experience and Williamson's correct analysis. We do deal with imposed ideas of success on so many levels that it becomes hard to see down the road to what extent they might have shaped our desire and choices. The further we go along with it, the easier it is for our ego to remain in the driver's seat. Ego is that false notion of self. But it doesn't just take over on its own. We allow thoughts, desires and actions to be governable and governed. However, this is not where we really miss the mark. We are even less willing to turn inward to our true heart's desires. We do know what it feels like to be off course, no matter how wonderful our lives look in the eyes of others.

The first step to success is recognizing to what extent our souls are being governed by our ego running after imposed ideas of success and all that glitters. If it feels oppressive deep within your core, it is oppressive no matter how much the ego tells you that you are doing great. To attach happiness to the attainment of material things is to set yourself up for failure, not success. Material things come and they go. Positions and prestige can be gone in a blink of an eye. We can avoid being trapped in this rat race by changing the definitions of success that are not in alignment with our soul's longing and purpose.

The next step is recognizing and embracing true success. True success is embodied no matter what happens in the world. True success is found within a source that has no beginning and no end and, therefore, no limit. It is found within and through ourselves. It is to experience the attainment of success in transcending the ego's wants for material gains, power, and outward recognition. It is to flow with the inner part of us that experiences the wealth of a growing and nourished soul. It is in this flow of the inner core in conjunction with that of Source, God, our Creator, and All That Is that abundance is truly known. Through this connection, abundance is real and there is no lack experienced. There is no void to fill because connection to Source is abundance lived.

This changes perspective and shifts your goals, how you pursue them and how you experience success. Career, for example, becomes the means for expressing your uniqueness, not the end goal. Worldly power is not the goal either, as then you will inevitably turn it into controlling power. Only inner power can be of the essence that empowers your life and that of others. Once you change your idea of success, you automatically shift goals so that they are aligned with deeper meaning and a larger purpose.

Throughout this book, you will learn the several essential keys to achieving *true* success. The first begins here with your new definition of it. Fundamentally, we need to shift our egocentric consumer attitude from needing and wanting 180 degrees to an outward flowing of giving. The other keys will be hard to use without this one. No more needing to have! Let it go. You already have what you need within you and through you. With our Creator we must step onto our path of giving. It is imperative that we recognize and live our purposes for why we are here. When we embrace this concept of success, we can begin to flow with a power of grace, intuition, and creativity. And here is the point—these serve to imbue forms with our unique energies in the best of possibilities. It is not magical but at the same time it is because by tapping into the highest part of our being we make things happen. Using the higher perspective gained through our soul we can only create the good.

Mistakes are not failures. They provide life lessons, whether you believe you created them or not. Even the ones you are sure you could never ever have chosen are there with purpose. Your soul has a higher awareness. Honor your lessons that come from mistakes and Divine orchestration because when you do they bestow upon you grace, flow, and direction. If you have many lessons to learn, you probably have a lot ahead of you to produce. Use them; they are meant to help you truly succeed.

*Begin Your Activism for Success*

You have things to do and little time to do it, so let's get to it because we all need your contribution. You will experience a new outcome from making this mental shift in your commitment to life and taking the right actions. When you truly manage to link into your intuition and work with a higher sense of being, you become less susceptible to stress, you feel healthier, happier, and easily rise above the need for material and worldly things. You easily have recognition that you have something special to offer. You do not have less at all! You are in sync with *real* success, so that if you lose all material possessions and outer acclaim, you know that you are still successful.

Now look at those who have been very wealthy and lost it or gave it away. Those who give freely of their genius and wealth not only experience success regardless of material goods, but they are also in a vibration that creates it over and over again in physical form. In this is much to reflect upon. Yet, as you work with the keys to success you will have a deeper knowing of success than can be conveyed through another's experience. In fact, this deeper knowing will free you of all the false notions of success that have kept you chained to other agendas, fears of people, or power structures.

*"Then you will know the truth and the truth shall set you free." (Jesus, in John 8:32)*

### Additional Message for Your Key To Success

When was the last time you listened to your
intuition, your heart, the part that makes you feel
alive? Change your routine for the rest of your day.
When you do that you are guidable. Your heart has
a chance to get through to you. True success, what
will really make you feel accomplished, is given
its chance through spontaneity. Go out and
enjoy a string of spontaneous acts. They will lead
you to recognize your heart's promptings and
perhaps its deepest desire.

~

# ⪗ 2 ⪗

# Key #2: Spiritual Intelligence

*Spiritual intelligence—the overarching framework encompassed at the soul level through which a higher meaning of life can be gained, the value of life's learning is perceived, and through which one is then able to choose the right actions that serve our ultimate purpose. To succeed in transforming absolutely anything in life requires being proactive with spiritual wisdom.*

## Introduction

Is it "logical" that we are not solving the host of increasing problems that are affecting us on a global scale? We are becoming more specialized in our studies and creating more advanced technologies. Does it make sense that highly educated and intelligent people are struggling to solve problems of a personal nature, tiny or large? Many people who have high IQs are simply unable to adequately deal with many of life's challenges even though they have great analytical abilities. It is really a shame that we cannot see that we continue to use the same methods and ways of thinking (albeit with some enhanced sophistication). Our inability to truly succeed has a continually wider global impact at the same time that our challenges are growing consistently more difficult.

Our skies are being polluted. But you didn't notice it often looks seriously different up there, did you? Among the numerous creatures going extinct, fish are dying out, and the ichthyologist who studies them—as one told me—would rather stop at a fast food restaurant than put the fish many of us are eating on his table. And in our drive to eradicate drugs and terrorists, has the world become any safer? No. We just continue doing what we are doing, justify it when need be, and keep rhetorically asking why all the hate? We are wrapped up in a momentum of great speed, heading into trouble and our intelligence alone can't wake us up to this reality. It really can't.

Despite all of our advancements, we are in trouble because of our narrow atomistic, de-compositional, linear, static approaches to absolutely everything from the personal to the political. This thinking comprises a tiny portion of the intelligence required to succeed at anything. To begin, I am convinced we are not fully using it. Yet, even if we did, analytical thinking alone will never be enough to transcend and transform the problems we have created or grasp the life lessons we are supposed to fully understand in order to succeed at life and in order to evolve. We require a higher way of thinking if we truly want to succeed, let alone survive.

### The Wrong With Analytical Thinking

We have it all wrong in diplomacy, public policy, organizational development, democratization, strategic management, business, law enforcement, counseling, the medical field, religious studies, defence—every social and scientific area. Experts, counselors, and scientists look at a problem or thing as a singular project. We don't notice that things affecting the problem come from within its environment. We don't give much thought to how those things are affecting other existences. We don't imagine that our own observation or interpretation of it might be affecting it.

The person that needs surgery, the organization that needs to do better, the criminal that needs to be straightened out is looked at as a solitary thing with clear boundaries. And because we have such a perspective, that thing and that thing alone becomes our project. Our only concern is how to fix it for today. In messing up with our project we forget that it or its progeny is going to play a role in the future. Nothing parallel is going on in the environment that will affect it tomorrow—no, we only worry about it today.

We approach the issue all wrong from every possible angle. We give it its specified time for analysis and fixing and no more. And we see only one level of it. We ignore its components and the important fact that its components have been influencing it, still are, and will continue to affect it somehow. Did we even wonder if this thing has a truly significant purpose let alone multiple significant purposes? What of its own consciousness and will? Because we fail to think broader and integrate the important stuff on all counts, its value is defined and limited. This is the analytical approach to life: limited.

We are given our mind to use. It is an organ that forms the decision center of the body. We hold within this organ the intelligence to calculate, weigh, and compute stored information. It also hosts memories that can be recalled when you are trying to make sense of something in the present that you think you have no knowledge to deal with. Our brain is a significant and wondrous resource. However, it is not where we primarily discern what is best for ourselves. Of course, you also gather as much information as is needed about a particular issue, being aware that information comes from various sources, experiences, interpretations, frameworks of thought, and agendas; however, the brain has never been, in my experience working with truly successful spiritual activists, the primary mode of operating. Nor do they rely on information acquired. The soul is the first guidance system.

## Mind and Soul

Logical reasoning is not an act entirely separate from the spirit despite the multi-various and established approaches to explaining spirituality, psychology and the mind. More often than not, we shut out guidance through an over-use of the rational part of our brain. However, more accurately, "Reason is a spark kindled by the beating of our heart" (Apocrypha: Wisdom of Solomon 2:2). We must align our thoughts with our heart, and our heart with a higher knowing. It is from a soul perspective of our purpose that we can recognize the meaning of our life lessons and identify the tools and strategies that will help us find and follow our straightest path.

There is ongoing change at ever-faster rates and with greater complexity. IQ alone won't get us through many real life challenges. Neither IQ nor our years specializing in our fields alone will help us solve conflicts or issues related to diplomacy or really anything that has an ethical, social, and moral dimension; indeed, anything that is related directly to the well-being of human beings. If our approaches resting on a general rational logical approach are failing us, then we need something more. We require an approach that is much more sophisticated.

However, because all things, including ourselves, have purposes, sophistication is not sufficient for success. Only an approach that encompasses purposefulness can offer any meaning and direction. Only an approach that works with universal laws governing all dimensions and systems will work. A system's inclusion of the soul is the only overarching approach that enables us to think, or rather know, on that higher level necessary for us to truly succeed at life.

A system's approach to the soul level of knowing provides us this perspective through spiritual intelligence. I define *spiritual intelligence* as the overarching framework encompassed at the soul level through which a higher meaning to life can be gained, the value of life's learning is perceived, and through which one is then able to choose the right actions that serve our ultimate purpose. Similarly, Robert Emmons defines spiritual intelligence as a framework for identifying and organizing the skills and competencies needed for the adaptive use of spirituality (Emmons, 1999, p. 163). Danah Zohar and Ian Marshall explain it as "the intelligence with which we solve problems of meaning and value, the intelligence with which we can place our actions and lives in a wider, richer, meaning-giving context, the intelligence with which we can assess that one course of action or life-path is more meaningful than another."[5] Importantly, it is also as Cindy Wigglesworth defines it: "The ability to behave with wisdom and compassion, while maintaining inner and outer peace, regardless of the situation."[6] Wigglesworth emphasizes that behavior is a key outcome of using this intelligence[7] and that developing the voice of your Higher Self (your soul) and learning how to follow its guidance is the most important part of spiritual intelligence.[8]

To succeed in transforming absolutely anything in life requires being proactive with spiritual wisdom. Spiritual activism is putting this key to use. The Association for Global New Thought views spiritual activism as "Spirit and Love put into action, and prayer made visible." Spiritual activism is creating change through bringing spirit, love and therefore light where needed through action. Spiritual activism is consciously using power and wisdom derived from connecting to our Creator to guide action for positive change. A spiritual activist attains success when using the soul's perspective, that is ultimately linked to and guidable by God, and taking concerted steps to achieve goals—action. The key to being leaders of light is to let light come through us to enlighten our lives and the world. For us to achieve this, our will must find constant alignment with God's will.

### Access Your Soul to Discern

In the times we made wrong choices, we can certainly recall a moment of decision before we went ahead with what we did. Perhaps you can remember some feeling prompted you to choose an alternative, that an alternative would show, or that the choice in front of you was but one of many choices. You knew before choosing that something did not *feel* right. That moment right there was your framework for guidance. It lets you know if your ego will is in alignment with your soul purpose and ultimately Divine will, or not.

We are all souls inhabiting a physical body. Our soul speaks to us through feelings, impressions, synchronicities, repetitions in our environment, what we tend to attract and repel, visions, dreams, or an intense knowing.

It is linked to many other frameworks and higher states, ultimately to our Creator. We are, for example, protected and guided by angels and guides that are in constant communication with the soul. There are really so many ways to know beyond using the brain.

We are always brought wisdoms for our highest success and straightest path through our soul. The universe, as an even more encompassing and higher system of intelligence, has a keen interest in each and every individual's ability to succeed in aligning with the Will of the Lord of all universes. The universe's system is purposeful, too. We are pushed and prompted to fulfill our individual and ultimate purpose through the heart. Our soul is purpose oriented with the highest objective of returning to its Creator. Therefore, it will provide you with the guidance needed and permitted to help you achieve your purposes in line with this ultimate purpose. The real work we have is to acknowledge and act on its wisdoms.

Through our heart we can quickly access a depth of knowing beyond any rational explanation. Tap into your inner or higher self to sense what leads to your well-being with every decision you make, from the mundane to large decisions. Just ask; we need only pray and we will be guided. You must listen. Guidance can fall on deaf ears. We need to calm our emotions and then sense in our gut or our heart if something feels right or it doesn't. You may get a feeling or impression. When this happens to you, acknowledge it. If appropriate, write it down or speak it out loud. Whatever you do, do not second-guess your heart's prompting and tugging. Acknowledge it because when you put it in your awareness, you give it its due value and when you give it value it becomes a consistently consciously present part of your guidance system.

We are constantly given external signs, symbols, and information to read and interpret. As Rumi says, "every external gives news of a hidden wisdom." You might, for example, ask for how to deal with someone you are in relationship with—a spouse, child, co-worker, parent, etc., and receive the answers in, for example, the form of a book that catches your attention. You might cross paths with a person who has dealt with the same problem and overcame it successfully and is glad to share her knowledge and wisdom. It is a tangible form and you were guided to it or it to you. Bring your awareness to present time so you don't miss these.

What this also means is that we are often seeing mirrored things in our lives that are trying to give us messages. Maybe we need to transform or purify something. We tend to dispense blame when things go wrong for us. The spiritually intelligent, however, look at things that are repeated as signs to make better choices for soul growth. If, for example, you keep running into the same type of partner or co-worker exhibiting the same personality traits or flaws, these are important for you to reflect upon. That person may well be difficult and the flaws may be real; however, if they repeat themselves, they also have something to say to you. They are reflecting something about you that needs attending to.

You cannot outwit your soul's intelligence for bringing these circumstances into your life by running from them. Your soul will not allow you to escape from your own expansion and your true success. It will constantly provide you the lesson you need in order to succeed. Whatever you are being shown, no matter how painful, never ever run, unless, of course, you are in harm's way. Take your focus off of the mistakes of others and discipline yourself to learn what imperfections you need to overcome. This is not passivity. It is action of immense courage and spiritual intelligence.

The more you allow your soul to come through you, the more you have from this essential source of power to help you discern which choices will enable your success. You are responsible for your choices, most of which will affect others, too, even if the choice for action started off creating a mere ripple. What better guidance than that of your soul created by and always connected to The Source, The Light, The All Knowing, The Truth, The Wise, The Guide.

*"The intellect of the wise is like glass; it admits the light of heaven and reflects it." (Augustus Hare)*

### Additional Message for Your Key To Success

These are times of great changes. It is important that you use your spiritual key of intuition and heavenly guidance every day. You already know the direction your heart is tugging you to move in. Take the first step today in listening to it. If you accept this invitation, your actions will set a course to a real experience of success. You will set courses for many, many others as they experience the ripple effect of your first step.

~

## ☞ 3 ☜

# Key #3: Energy Vibrations

*Not only can we sense the different energetic vibrations and become affected by them; we affect the vibrations in a room or any environment. Just as we have the ability to spark, engage, or prolong lower ways of behaving and being, we can empower, lighten, brighten, and raise all that is around us for the better.*

## Introduction

Everything in the universe, from the rock on the ground to the person in front of you, to the planet Saturn, has a particular and unique vibration. This vibration is related to the frequency within the object or entity, the speed of which is also affected by its environment. The frequency determines whether the object or entity has a heavy, often inconsistent and slow vibration, or a light, usually consistent and high vibration. Because the object is connected to its surroundings, it has an effect on its environment as well and it is simultaneously affected by objects within the field surrounding it. Inevitably, it attracts what is vibrating at the same frequency as itself. This is significant if we think about what we as individuals might be attracting into our everyday lives, as well the things we desire but are actually repelling.

## Quantum Physics and Vibrations

Today, many quantum physicists (among other scientists) recognize that everything has a particular resonance and that these objects or bodies have their own consciousness. This is important for understanding energetic frequency and the role of frequencies in our ability to relate to others. Earth rotates within an electromagnetic field, which is connected to All That Is within it and all outside it. Just as the sun or our planet Earth is swirling with energy, connected to the cosmos in intricate balance, other objects and life forms are pulsing with energy and forming part of the same matrix of energy. We are part of an energetic system where the body, mind, emotions, and spirit are all part of our makeup as just one aspect of our universe's system.

While some scientists stopped short where the theory has not managed to explain the results of some fascinating experiments on matter in our universe, others are continuing to research the idea that subatomic particles may be considered as vibrating strings. In quantum physics, gravity is mediated by a particle of zero mass, called the graviton. The theory took major steps forward when it was discovered that the lowest vibration of strings describes such a particle. In 1995, Edward Witten found that the strings vibrate not within our familiar four-dimensional space-time but in multiple dimensions, whereby he found 11.[9]

## Understanding Energy Vibrations

Fear, hate, and jealousy are comprised of heavy vibrations. These states within a person are low frequency. When a person is absorbed in any one or a mixture of these feelings, he is vibrating in a low state. He not only feels negative emotions, but his body and mind are also in sync with this vibratory state. When within this vibratory state, it becomes difficult for him to feel calmness and at one with life. When this happens, he is mentally sending out messages that produce vibrations of the same frequency in his environment. Spiritually, he is not going to lift anyone up that he crosses paths with. Emotionally, he is sending off feelings that will sooner or later spark someone else's state so that potential for negative engagement with a person is present.

Have you ever walked down a street with someone who is deeply fearful of dogs? Perhaps you are the one who has a fear of dogs and walked together with someone who has next to no fear of these animals. What happened when a guard dog or a dog that appeared scary came towards you? Most likely, it checked out the one person who was beyond himself in fright and barked aggressively or actually attacked! The frequency of fear attracts a like vibration of aggression. The dog chose the person who was scared because of the numerous signals that this person sent out. A person does not have to look scared or visibly shake to be detected as fearful, as evinced through the use of lie detector tests. However, the dog can be coming from afar and already *know* which person within the group is exuding fear.

Love, humour, joy, and peace are comprised of light energetic vibrations. What does it feel like when you walk into a classroom where youngsters have just had joyous playtime? Undoubtedly, if you stand and let yourself feel the vibrations in the room, you will be tickled with the energies remaining in that room. What does it feel like when entering a room after some people just had a fight there? Fiery emotions are also low vibrating and inconsistent. There will likely be a notable difference between the feelings you sense in this room and the one in which children were just playing.

Not only can we sense the different energetic vibrations and become affected by them; we affect the vibrations in a room or any environment. Just as we have the ability to spark, engage, or prolong lower ways of behaving and being, we can empower, lighten, brighten, and raise all that is around us for the better. A small shift in frequency is often all that is required to change sadness to peace, fear to joy, and the many challenging situations we humans will face to a whole different reality.

What does understanding energy vibrations do for your ability to succeed? Vibration is a basic source of power that offers you infinite possibilities. A mother may be able to influence her baby to rest more peacefully if she sings a soothing song to it with the warmth of her heart. A person can dissipate his friend's anger by mentally directing his friend's venting to bounce away while focusing on sending his friend loving feelings as confirmed with positive words. Ultimately, these choices provide vibrations that affect one's self-esteem, one's relationships, and therefore one's ability to create change in the world.

To effectively use this source of power, you have to remember that it is not words, but rather feelings, attitudes, and beliefs that encompass communication on wavelengths. These feelings, attitudes, and beliefs can be formed within low frequencies all the way in the spectrum to high frequencies. The higher the frequency, the more light you are able to bring to your surroundings. Even if you represent a tiny light in what seems like an enormous cave of darkness, your light will pierce through. To tap into this source of power you need to be aware of your feelings and thoughts and guard them to ensure they are operating within a high frequency.

### How to Raise Your Vibrations

There are a number of ways to raise your vibration. First, recognize who you are. You are a soul and spirit in a human body, and your soul and spirit are beautiful and radiant. Not only do we receive guidance through the system of the soul, but we also receive light energy. When you remember this, you will know how much of a resource you already are. Radiate your soul light into this world through the vehicle God gave you. The vibration originating from your soul is unique and like no other. The qualities of its light radiate out in a way that no other person is capable. When you anchor yourself in the knowledge of your soul's presence, you are able to live your life with humility, generosity, integrity, and faith. This self-knowledge alone transcends other identities the ego often attaches to. This self-knowledge helps others around you raise their vibrations.

Forgive! Forgiveness is the most relieving and compassionate act known to mankind. Not forgiving is keeping yourself chained to pain many times more than the person you consciously or subconsciously want to continue holding accountable. You actually torture yourself, not really the other person, when you hold onto the memory of some past action and perhaps the anger that is attached to that memory. When you forgive, you are actually releasing pent up low vibrating energy that is eating at your insides. You then permit yourself to live in peace. The person who wronged you might have forgotten what he did to you long ago.

Forgive yourself. If you carry guilt, ask yourself if it is over something that cannot be changed. If it cannot be changed, learn what that situation has to offer you but then move forward. Forgive yourself. When you forgive yourself you actually enable yourself to not repeat what caused you to feel guilty. On the other hand, when you hold onto your guilt you actually hold yourself in the energy of its vibration that makes it easier for you to repeat the same action. Forgiving frees. You raise your vibrations manifold and produce an energetic effect that elicits a capacity to be merciful and compassionate.

Give love. Love is the highest vibration. Ultimately, love is from Source and it is limitless. When we acknowledge who we are, embrace our connection to God, and allow love to flow through us, we are raising our own vibration and all that is around us in the most intense way possible. Then when we offer it, we dissolve pain in the heart, firstly our own. No matter what is going on around you or who wronged you, keep loving. Continue giving love and you will reap love in your life.

Do something fun. Most of us get into a rut in doing our chores and carrying out our responsibilities. Most of us are thinking about what is going to happen tomorrow or what went wrong in the past. Move out of repetition of a singular reality and non-realities. Through doing activities that raise your spirits, you are getting in touch with your inner tugging of desire, the energy that pushes you to embody your highest essence. Doing things that excite you leaves you feeling fresh, alive, and full of energy.

Live life. We all have downs. They will pass. Do not let them hold you back from living. Through living life, you are giving from your life. Find the activities that first enable you to live life so that you can continue to give, even when circumstances are difficult. These could be walking in nature, swimming, listening to an uplifting program, reading a spiritual book, painting, writing, singing, gardening, or having a rendezvous with your spouse. These activities help take you out of the thoughts in your head that are creating all sorts of false interpretations of your situation and bring you to the present moment. They get you to feel what life is offering you in the present moment. They ultimately help you to express yourself out into the world on higher wavelengths despite all the ups and downs of life.

Be mindful of your purpose. Remembrance of your spiritual path and the point that our life circumstances are there to guide us to and on our path automatically places you in higher vibrations. You can be in remembrance through tapping into your deeper knowing or connecting through ritual. When you pray, mediate, or visualize, you are opening up to higher vibrations. Being in connection, you are able to center yourself in the vibrations of peace and calm. Connection creates the ability to link into the vibration of faith. Faith in turn enables you to become more conscious of the knowing of your soul and the wisdoms behind your life lessons.

When you learn to switch to higher vibrations, you are the master of your experience. You have greater power to choose how you will feel and act. When you are feeling great after a jog through a park and then someone complains to you, do you feel miserable or are you more able to brush it off, maybe listen, or give advice, if need be? Choosing to switch to a higher energetic frequency is a major key to success because it puts you in the driver's seat. You are less susceptible to the effects of others' dramas and negative outlooks. When you are centered in your own being, you have a greater capacity to look beyond life's ups and downs with clarity and purpose. Instead of being affected negatively, you can affect others and situations positively. You are better able to see the wisdoms of life's tests and learn from them faster. You are a significant instrument for change.

*"Be careful of your moods and feelings, for there is an unbroken connection between your feelings and your visible world."* (Neville Goddard)

### Additional Message for Your Key To Success

Look at what you have in your environment with
thankfulness. You are receiving more abundance
through this vibration of gratitude. Reflect on the
abundance of the universe. Acknowledge
it is your birthright to flow with prosperity in
your life. You are now receiving
greater prosperity
and abundance.

∾

## ≈ 4 ≈

# Key #4: Interdependence

*Each particle within an energetic system affects its whole, which
is part of a larger whole. When you create good things, you
raise that ability in others by direct influence. When your family
lives a life of peace and integrity, your community is affected.
The world is affected.*

## Introduction

One of the biggest ways we can sabotage our dreams is
by believing the myth that independence is key to success. The notion that "self-made" individuals got to
where they are through hard work truly independently
of all others is difficult to justify. Independence is a vir-
tue insofar as we strengthen ourselves, our physical, mental, emotional, and spiritual parts, to become whole and
functional. When we are whole and functional we are
better equipped to choose where we want to be and discern whether where we will be is for the good of all. Yet,
to get to the highest levels of our potential and that of
humanity, we will also never do it alone.

## Interdependence as Planetary Ethic

We are affected by and affect each other. Our fate is intricately connected. Choosing *interdependence* is a higher principle than independence. It is one of the major sources of power, without which we will not succeed, let alone survive. We need to choose it because it helps us achieve more. Interdependence is a higher principle because it is how the universe functions and to go against how the universe operates can only present one with difficulty, pain, and increased sense of insecurity.

Science has now shown us the wholeness of all parts to the universe. Recently, quantum scientists have been able to better understand the discovery that 96 percent of the universe is comprised of dark matter. What has been established amongst many leading quantum physics scientists through a famous experiment now run thousands of times is the entangled nature of twin particles. The nonlocality of quantum entities (quanta refers to the particles that were thought of as the building blocks of material reality and which turned out to be more like waves than tiny particles) shows that the universe is innately whole.[10]

We are part of an energetic system where the body, mind, emotions, soul, and spirit are part of a whole. Furthermore, our own energetic system is linked to our brother's system, our neighbour's, the person all the way on the other side of the globe, and beyond. Beyond includes every particle from which our "accepted" systems have evolved!

As a planetary ethic this puts us in a whole different ballgame in understanding that success is not an individual consequence or a result of fate. Success must be sought with this ethic as a central guidepost. If we

succeed to have something but take it away from someone else, we will eventually feel some form of loss because
we are interconnected. We live in a universal community
sharing its broader existence and experience, just as the
individual cells make up an organ and ultimately the individual body. A Native American saying goes, "The hurt
of one is the hurt of all, the honor of one is the honor of
all." There is no separation.

We are part of an entire cosmos that is interdependent and interconnected. This means that we are not
only connected to each and every human we think of
as good or bad, but we are also one with all of creation.
Albert Einstein had described:

> A human being is a part of a whole, called by us
> 'universe,' a part limited in time and space. He
> experiences himself, his thoughts and feelings as
> something separated from the rest . . . a kind of
> optical delusion of his consciousness. This delusion
> is a kind of prison for us, restricting us to our per-
> sonal desires and to affection for a few persons near-
> est to us. Our task must be to free ourselves from
> this prison by widening our circle of compassion to
> embrace all living creatures and the whole of nature
> in its beauty.

Not long ago I sat in on and moderated a session
(which, I might add, I failed) at a conference in London
made up of mostly political scientists, religious preachers
from the major religions, and activists. I was pleasantly
surprised to listen to two speakers from the Grameen
Bank talk about the interconnectedness of human beings
and challenge the attendees to imagine the consequences

of this fact. They consisted of the first speakers. When the topic of Iraq came up, one of the following speakers pointed his finger at an Iraqi Orthodox Christian preacher on the panel and the whole session became deluded back into separatist thinking which then culminated into aggressive remarks shot back and forth with an increased volume of willing participants.

While I do see this case representing the adage "one step forward, two steps back," we need to seriously ask why do we continue to have difficulty putting the conceptual knowledge of our oneness into securing its wholeness in practice? Separatist thinking in Iraq between an increasing number of groups has only caused the country to spiral into greater chaos and bloodshed. I am afraid the separatist thinking and terror in its invasion can only bear its consequences of a wider scale if oneness is not embraced very soon on a planet-wide view.

### Are We Moving Toward Living Interdependence?

How many movies, shows, and video games do we expose ourselves and our impressionable children to that nail in the message firmly: to choose depending on ourselves? We have to believe in the myth of isolation and self-sufficiency if that is what is constantly in front of us. It is obvious many of us do because there are numerous examples of individuals acting in ways toward others that are harmful and irresponsible beyond a politically oriented conference setting. Others carry out their day-to-day activities without any passing thought for others' needs, poverty, oppression, or worse. These happen within our own communities—even in our own homes. Long-term success will never be achieved this way.

As with the above example, some governments have done superbly to link self-sufficiency and isolation with security. Polls in the U.S. prove it. Individuals among nearly all nations are told that the security and identity of their nation is dependent upon the ability to be militarily, educationally, and culturally independent of other nations. Much in the same way, this systematic call to isolation is tearing communities once living in peace entirely apart in ethnic, civil, or gang wars. The overall idea is that we are separate and dependent upon our own top-down initiatives; furthermore, that those in positions of authority among us will ensure our survival and security. There could be nothing more delusional.

The media and political programs can be successful—momentarily—because they pull the strings of our fear vibrations. They manage to get deep into us because, like playing an instrument, they play on the vibrations of fear, jealousy, greed, and hate. It is we, however, who are at fault when we allow ourselves to be directed in whatever direction desired by such programs of acute interest and calculation. What sells more than the very films that work on our ego forms? We are told what fear, love, and success means—we are paying handsome sums to be told lies, yes, albeit with some entertainment, but the underlying principles for success we are fed are upside down.

The farther we have strayed from our path, the more we are disconnected from the light. The more we are disconnected and isolated, the weaker we are. When we have separated ourselves from humanity and from God, we desperately grab for something to fill the vacuum of emptiness left within our being. When we can no longer feel and we are numb to our soul, we dwell within the confines of ego. It is no mystery how the disconnected succumb to programs of manipulation. Unfortunately, as a result, we are making insufficient effort to take action against manipulative political and economic programs.

## The Value of Connecting

When one is united with life forces, one is united with life. It is a choice that you make to achieve real success. A person who makes this choice can build something better than he would be able to alone and has the potential to make that thing larger and stronger. Interdependence creates not weakness but strength.

What is the significance of tapping into the resource of interconnection and interdependence? Differences in colour, race, sex, religious affiliation, skills and educational achievement, jobs, etc. are as they are so that we may honor and celebrate them. At the basic level, we are asked to revere uniqueness. These differences make up both who we are and highlight what we can offer. Once we are able to appreciate our uniqueness and that we all come from the same Creator, we can take the next step to having reverence for all things made. We each have the spark of light as blown into all that is created with consciousness through His angels. This connects us with the Divine and connects all of us with all of His creation. The key is to recognize and embrace all of creation because we all share the same essence and we all have the same ultimate purpose of returning to our Creator. Because our ultimate goal is shared, to step on a person or aspect of the created pulls us back on a spiritual level and we experience the consequences on a material level.

As Ervin Laszlo explains, unicellular systems—the basic building blocks of our own systems that we normally give no thought to—began by forming colonial organisms from which specialization then created a collective system. From these, life forms of multicellular organisms have sprouted that inhabit our earth on the more developed spectrum of life as plants and animals. Laszlo, thus, argues, "In a planetary ethic reverence for this variety of system is expressed in the attribution of intrinsic value: value for such systems in themselves, regardless of their relation to and utility for other systems."[11] Hence, Laszlo declares, "In a planetary ethic individual human beings as well as the communities formed by human beings qualify for intrinsic value."[12]

Here is where this planetary ethic serves you. If your spouse, a co-worker, child, parent, pet, or neighbour is diminished in your eyes, look for the good. It is there and because it was created by the same God as you and I were, it possesses the same essence and has the same intrinsic value. Each individual life is sacred. Since you are connected, when you focus on the good, praise, and nurture it, you therefore expand it. This ethic in all your intentions and actions serves you in that the good in you will grow and expand, too. It is universal law that what you give is what you get.

"Do onto your brother (or neighbour) as you would want done to yourself" is a principle within all religions. This means you place yourself in the shoes of the other and imagine what experiences might feel like to that person. It means feeling for the rock, the plant, the earth, the bird, the tiger, the family member, the neighbour, or a person in another locality or country who you know is experiencing some hardship. You really are not separated even though materially you seem to be. You have something to offer, whether kind words, a smile, information, experience, a blanket, money, or your mere presence. What you give, in fact, will come back to you multiplied.

Choosing interdependence impacts your ability to succeed far beyond the mere material level. It is the resource for survival, growth, evolution, and expansion for each individual and the whole system of which we are a tiny part. The loving couples are comprised of two separate souls and are not responsible for the others' actions. The enemies are not responsible for each other's choices. However, each individual, although not responsible for another individual's deeds or misdeeds, must work in the way of moving her larger "organism" to the right actions. This is because as one organism all individuals have a stake in the same fate in accordance to the accumulated actions of the individual, community, or nation.

What quantum physics has enabled us to further understand, in using the principle of interdependence, is the non-locality of our actions. When we tap into the force that binds us together, we create change not only within ourselves and not only within our homes. When you change yourself, every family member in your home must change too because we are all connected at the sub-atomic level. When you choose to live a life of grace and compassion, your family members will follow your example. However, you will influence them via a shift in your energy that on the quantum level has automatically created a shift within their own energetic system.

Each particle within an energetic system affects its whole, which is part of a larger whole. When you create good things, you raise that ability in others by direct influence. When your family lives a life of peace and integrity, your community is affected. The world is affected. Choosing to work with the law of interdependence is one of the most profound and simple ways to create success that affects each individual and each system within the mind of the broader cosmos.

> *"Humankind has not woven the web of life. We are but one thread within it. Whatever we do to the web, we do to ourselves. All things are bound together. All things connect." (Chief Seattle, 1854)*

### Additional Message for Your Key To Success

Continue to give gratitude. When you are in a
state of gratitude, you strengthen your connection
with Creator. You become aware of your
connection with all that is created. Feel the joy of
gratitude. When you do, you have an even deeper
recognition of the interdependence of all
things. You recognize the vast and
inexhaustible abundance of
the universe.

∽

## ≈ 5 ≈

# Key #5: The Law of Attraction

*The law of attraction states that like attracts like. When an object vibrates at a particular resonance, it pulls into its existence those objects that have a similar resonance.*

## Introduction

In her book, *A Little Light on the Spiritual Laws*, Diana Cooper reminds us about the experience of young children playing with magnets. As children, we are learning about the world through little fascinating experiments. Many of us were once intrigued with the observation that magnets can cling together, repel each other and when held in different positions, display no reaction. Cooper reminds us that life works in the same manner—we attract some people or situations, and repel others. Some situations are simply not pulled into orbit because we have not provided the magnetic pull.

People who are truly successful in attracting what they desire in life do not lose touch with the inner inquisitiveness about the world. In adulthood people tend to forget how fascinating life can be at the workings of a basic source of power. We have buried this basic wisdom of universal law through our acquired belief systems.

We just take what other people tell us about the way the world works. When they say the world is about limitations that we must accept, we resign ourselves to their limited understanding, too. But we can learn how to create our own experience of success through the law of attraction.

## Importance of Connection to the Wider World

Most individuals have lost touch with connection to the wider world and their purpose. Here is one way. Some who talk on the law of attraction ask that we do not peer into this darkness but rather focus on the good in this world. This needs clarification. We must recognize the dark to know what is the light. We need to be fully aware of all that exists. It is correct that *focusing* on darker realities does not make us successful. It keeps us wallowing in limited thinking. But from there we can get clear about where we want to go. If you refuse to look at your weaknesses, how do you think you can realistically evaluate ways to improve? Denial, ignorance, and dreamy ideas of positivity comprise the recipe for failure.

If you refuse to tune into world news or happenings in your community, you might miss opportunities to learn about people who are struck with some calamity and could use help from those who are now informed. This is besides the fact that news sources are biased and often manipulative. The point is that the erroneous idea of keeping positive by ignorance does not help advance your soul evolution or the betterment of humanity at all. With an overview of where you can do something and the spectrum of possibilities to do something, we can then focus with clarity on that route. In fact, being knowledgeable and aware of what needs fixing not only orients us to alternatives but also should motivate us to create the change needed.

Importantly, if we do not peer into the darkness we become detached from the emotions that motivate human beings to right action and service. Without feeling the darkness, we detach from our brothers and sisters who really are experiencing pain, sometimes at depths we will never be able to truly know in our lifetime. Awareness of our own dark sides and awareness of the plight of those we are physically and spiritually interdependent with, forms the basis from which we can be in touch with the vibrations of acceptance, forgiveness, love and compassion. These are the vibrations that heal us and heal others.

## How the Law of Attraction Works

The law of attraction states that like attracts like. When an object vibrates at a particular resonance, it pulls into its existence those objects that have a similar resonance. When it vibrates differently than another object, the other object simply occupies a different space. The same applies to all things, including people. People whose frequency is different than our own are not attracted to us. We are made up of a particular frequency, as are all things having a molecular structure. Even inanimate objects have their own frequency. Thoughts and feelings we have, such as fear, greed, anger, and jealousy, as well neediness, dependency, or desperation, send out pulses of energy of low frequency. If any of these make up a consistent characteristic in a person, she is bound to attract someone with similar vibrations. On the other hand, if our character traits include faithfulness, generosity, joy, compassion, and love, we must attract a person into our life who similarly has these qualities.

I knew someone who would write on the topic of racism and violence. I gathered he had an extreme fixation on violence when, while I was working with him, he further insisted that I see proof of the development of a book he was co-authoring with a notorious killer behind bars on shared childhood experiences of violence. He had experienced violence as a result of racism many times from childhood until then. I was able to verify his violent experiences in a more recent case where he took legal action through another organization with which I was affiliated. In addition, over a four-month period in which I was in communication with him, he was violently attacked twice, and so badly and in a place considered safe that there was a write up of the incident in the leading national newspaper. Certainly, he did not deserve any of these experiences and he suffered a great deal at the hands of racist individuals. However, I perceive a certain frequency and his fearful attention to violent acts may have repeatedly brought them into his reality.

Most law of attraction theorists believe we attract absolutely everything we experience. As I will demonstrate below, this is simply not true. I have been slammed with some sudden new experience in the midst of feeling vibrationally in a different space and in my thoughts a completely different realm. This is where such experiences come from: our soul together with God has chosen it. Our soul has awareness of the purposes of many circumstances in which we will find ourselves.

*Attracting Situations for Life Lessons*

The system of the soul is determined to fulfill the purpose of a Higher will. In that higher sense, a circumstance may be brought into our lives. These circumstances are in such case predestined to serve our choice for soul growth, expressing ourselves in higher ways through the experience, and sometimes the growth of others.

However, it is important to be aware that vibrations can also be a significant factor. This is not bad news; it allows for the possibility to influence not only our experiences but also the circumstances that give rise to experiences. What we attract that is felt as painful and perceived as negative serves that which we take responsibility to choose as alternative thinking, feeling, and acting that will bring us greatest success.

Success is gained through learning. We attract like into our lives as a way of learning. If a woman, for example, realizes that she is sharing her life with people who are physically abusive, she needs to honestly ask herself why she attracted these individuals into her life if she wishes to break the pattern. Even if she is not outwardly abusive, there is some quality within her that she is not dealing with. Often she is suppressing anger in a way that her actions are passive-aggressive or even passive, so that a relationship dynamic comes into play in which one is the aggressor and the other is the enabler.

More often than not, the woman who endures a relationship with a man who is physically abusive and leaves without understanding this dynamic or is dumped, will run straight into the next relationship characterized again by the same dynamics of abuse. That is, if she does not work on herself to change the quality within her that is attracting an abusive partner. Certainly, as well, she does not deserve ill treatment and, unquestionably, she should physically remove herself and her children from any such dangerous situation. However, she attracted it in her life in the first place in order to address the thing about her, some character flaw, so that she can change it and develop spiritually, mentally, and emotionally. Successful at that, she is bound to do better next time around if she chooses to get into a relationship and live a life of greater peace, or accomplish something else for which she needed this clearing.

That is why it is so essential to embrace our dark sides. We all have them and we share them in humanity. It takes courage to look at them. To turn away from them because they are deemed "negative" is cowardice. The woman who accepts that she bears responsibility for being in a relationship with a man who abuses her strengthens herself. She is stronger than the person who denies he has a problem and blames everybody else for his bad relationships and bad life circumstances. There is no comparison. Not only does a person who refuses to learn his lessons run into the same problem over and over again, but the problems also become magnified. This is the universe's way of making it loud and clear that he needs to change course to be successful at life.

The law of attraction facilitates a means by which we grow because the tests of attracting something that does not feel good or is in fact harmful to us pushes us to do what we need to in order to feel good from within and to desire the good qualities that bring joy. As Rumi states, "suffering is a treasure, for it contains mercies." Grasping the key of attraction is empowering yourself to move forward in life. It is immensely empowering to know that we can have what we want and that God wants us to have the good.

*Working with the Law of Attraction*

The law of attraction can be directed to many different goals. However, for success to be experienced, it must be used in attracting good in our environment for the good of all and the harm of none. When we desire something and aim to attract it, we must remember that to take it away from someone else does not serve humanity, let alone our own soul development. Before choosing to attract something into our lives, we need to consider if going after that thing, whether a job, a person, a house, or land, will violate some right or a sense of "compassionate justice." Compassion, integrity, unconditional love, and morality are conditions that must be met while aiming to attract something we desire in order for success to be truly experienced.

To ensure long term success, we seek alignment with our soul purpose and Divine will. If we begin with asking ourselves what our true motives and intentions are, we can best align our vibrations with what serves our highest good. Ask, "Will achieving _____ help me live my purpose or take me away from it?" "What is my heart telling me on this?" God wants us to have the good and joy in our lives and if we surrender to align our vibrations with receiving our highest good, we will experience greater flow towards that which brings us real success and happiness. What we are meant to have and offer is first planted in the heart.

Successfully using the law of attraction requires that you give it time. Often what we desire to have takes time to become our reality. You need to remain in a spiritual space of gratitude and patience for the lessons this phase is giving you. You can assist this phase by continuously giving thanks for the opportunities of this period. Gratitude expands your vibrations in order to move into the energies of higher frequencies. You can facilitate it by opening your eyes, mind, and heart to your yearning to learn and grow. Once we have learned the lessons from our situations, we enter a new vibrational space. It is as if we enter the bottleneck of the bottle when we feel stuck, constrained, and squeezed by life. But then with patience and endurance we are pushed into joy, freedom, and even greater expansion.

You vibrate with that thought and send out messages in line with the vibration of that thought. If there is a thought that is not what you want to lead to manifestation, such as, "I'm not good enough for the promotion," then eliminate that thought by replacing it with the positive, i.e., "I am good enough and the promotion is right for me." When you see yourself as worthy, deserving of the good, and you are faithful that you are always being taken care of, you raise your vibrations to step into the bounty that God, Source, The Provider, All That Is has ready for your taking. When you live in higher frequencies of love and faith, you develop spiritually and enjoy the blessings that must be attracted with those vibrations.

> "We think in secret and it comes to pass. Our environment is but a looking glass." (James Allen)

### *Additional Message for Your Key to Success*

You have attracted situations in your life right
now. They are there to assist you in the growth
that you need at this particular time. You
are meant to experience your full
potential. Take time out to reflect on
one situation. Celebrate your growth
thus far. Remove those thoughts
that are not working for you
anymore. Replace them with
higher, more positive
thinking. You are now
attracting your
even higher
potential.

∾

## ≈ 6 ≈

# Key #6: Purification

*The soul yearns for cleansing and expanding. It is assigned a purpose to continually grow. Before growth can happen, we usually need to release something or clear some habit or pattern. Cleansing and purifying is part of the essential process of soul growth and the evolution of humanity.*

## Introduction

What does purification have to do with your ability to succeed? A tremendous deal. We will never succeed at attaining our highest goals or be able to transform difficult situations if we are burdened with baggage. I am speaking of the baggage and clutter we hold within ourselves that keep us from evolving into our highest expressions. Purification is the prerequisite for growth. Fortunately, we will be given opportunities to cleanse away that within us which is not serving us on our path. This is spiritual law. Accumulated negative habits over time, problematic personality traits, and dipping into low vibrations give rise to a process called purification.

Whether we think we have major baggage or are doing pretty well, we need to undergo purification habitually throughout our lives. The signs start to show up in

our lives in various ways. These can be difficult circumstances that serve as reminders that we need to release
that which needs releasing. When we cleanse ourselves
of dysfunction, we experience lightness and greater connection to the spiritual realm. In purifying we attain the
key to materially manifest what we aim for. We can see
tangible results as things in our life start to fall back into
place or take better adaptations.

*Opening to Life Lessons*

No test presented to us in life is beyond what we as
unique individuals can manage. Even when something
has caused more pain than we have ever imagined possible, our capacities are known and we are given sources of
power to pull ourselves back from the situation. As in all
mystical teachings and as is universally exact, it is promised that God does not burden any human being with
more than He/She[13] has given him.

A situation will mirror something within us that
needs to be dealt with or to be purged. It can take the
form of people criticizing us about some aspect of ourselves or we experience subtle situations where we are
stopped to think. Think about the times you are driving
in a hurry and just at that very time you need to have the
road open the traffic is horrendous. Maybe you need to
slow down in other areas of your life to gift yourself the
time to reflect and spiritually connect. Maybe someone in
your life, a parent, spouse, or child, wants desperately to
connect with you, and especially at this time.

It is important that when the universe is showing us
something that is within us, our shadow part, we embrace
it and not project it onto some outside thing. It is not the

row of cars ahead of you in a traffic jam that is the real problem. Yes, there is a row of cars and you would like to drive on, but there is a message in that for you. We tend to place blame on something or somebody. This would be an example for reflection, growth, and often working through and letting go of something.

The soul yearns for cleansing and expanding. It is assigned a purpose to continually grow. Before growth can happen, we usually need to release something or clear some habit or pattern. Each time we move through one of the life lessons we often get rid of something that we either brought upon ourselves or can no longer see a purpose for. Cleansing and purifying this is part of the essential process of soul growth and the evolution of humanity.

*Strategies for Purification*

Removing what no longer serves us or holds us back from following our highest path takes consistency, discipline, and deliberate strategies. It does not matter whether these are negative character flaws, habits, trains of thought, or various other forms of being, we need to use disciplined action to purify them. There are a number of ways that you can support your purification.

We sometimes rely on or work with another person for help with the purification process. You can aid the process by seeking out a counselor or therapist. A skilled practitioner can support your releasing of old patterns and eventual growth by helping you work through your life challenge. He or she will be effective if an integral approach is included in the therapy that appreciates the influence of the different levels of being.

A spiritual teacher who uses some modality of healing or teaching should also be able to assist you to move through whatever it is you're facing with greater ease and spiritual intelligence. But be selective in doing spiritual work with others. As with any type of therapist, whatever healing your teacher is specialized in, the desired outcome is to be able to shift your perspective even if ever so slightly, so that purifying, healing, and future work is sustainable.

Find the company of people who have the clearest energies. People who practice a positive approach to life are generally clearer. This is a simple method but can work well. Some of your own energies will automatically be cleansed by proximity. The process occurs through the influence of higher ways of acting. Numerous studies have shown that whatever trait you wish to emulate can be gained through involving yourself with those people who exemplify them.

Removing what no longer serves you includes foremost auditing your energetic frequency. It takes constant practice, not just when we move through life challenges. When you get angry, for example, you may release pent up emotions. But that might only feel good for the short term. Likely you have lower vibrating energies around you and in the room you need to clear. If you do not, they will affect you and others. When we leave our homes and enter the various spaces with others where we may subject ourselves to lower vibrations, we need to cleanse our energies of these lower vibrations that may have seeped into our own or drained from ours. Sometimes the energy in our own homes needs clearing.

Although your energetic frequency may be compromised in various ways, raising your vibration and cleansing it are two different things. You can raise your vibration after, for example, you have come into contact with a person who is excessively negative. Energetic transmission has occurred whereby that person probably not only took some of your energy, but also left you with some of theirs; even on a subtle level you will have bits of energetic dirt remaining on your energetic body.

More people turn to vibrational therapies. These methods also purify the energetic body around the physical body. They work on the spiritual, emotional, mental, and physical layers of the whole person. That is why they are also called holistic therapies. They consider the whole makeup of a person, not just what most people see as the physical body. Sometimes people who have mental or emotional issues they have dealt with over an extended period will begin to see physical manifestations in some form of ailment within their bodies. This is because every aspect of the body is connected. The mental aspect affects the physical, as well as the emotional and spiritual. If a person is addicted to drugs, chemical imbalances not only occur but also emotional and spiritual imbalances. Recent studies indicate that heart problems are linked to emotional inclinations exhibited by what is referred to as A type personalities, workaholics, or overly ambitious people.

Your own thoughts and beliefs can serve to limit and cause damage. Thoughts, however, are also vibrations. Keep a mental note of your thoughts on a continuous basis. You will affect your energies with negativity, fear, guilt, and hate if you do not keep them in check. Denying these emotions will not help you purge them but acknowledging them as part of being human and embracing them will.

If anger is pervading your thoughts and actions, allow yourself to feel what it is you are angry about. Sincerely ask yourself, "What am I so angry about?" Allow yourself to see the mental pictures of what you think is causing the anger. Usually, something or someone did not meet your expectations. Perhaps something is happening that you are unable to control and wish you could. Try to see its cause from other angles with compassion for yourself and those you have mentally placed in the scene.

Be patient; purging often comprises a process. Sometimes you may need to feel the pain underlying the anger more deeply before you are ready to let it go. You also need to integrate on all levels the change that is occurring. So, for example, if mentally you can see a situation from another angle you might need to allow yourself some time to digest this new view emotionally. It is not always necessary but having been in the place of an old reality can require time to adjust to a new one.

It is wise to purge layer by layer. So, to deal with the anger, you can assist the mental layer by working on the spiritual through prayer or by increasing faith in the Divine. You can simultaneously purge through simple physical exercise. Exercise releases toxins within the cells that hold energetic imprints of the situation fed by the neurons by mental activity of thought formation.

Exercise also releases sedative hormones that simultaneously decrease the secretion of other hormones. Decreasing these other hormones biologically is important because some of these carry the peptides that have been prompting angry emotions, thereby causing a vicious cycle of experiencing anger and then having the need to feel anger again. When a decrease in those peptide-carrying hormones is supported, and especially when replaced with calming hormones in the bloodstream, the body is able to support healthy and balanced emotions and the energetic vibrations they emit.

## Elemental Forces for Purification

Fire, water, air, and earth serve as powerful tools for purification. Many scientists have attested to the power of fire as a cleanser and rejuvenator. When forests are burned to ashes, from under the soot emerge fresh life unburdened by deadening or rotten parts. Some forms of plant life do not grow except under the condition of fires. More essentially, fire transmutes lower energies into higher forms. Burning cleansing essences in the home are useful.

Swimming in a lake or ocean is also very powerful as a cleanser and, again, specifically when done with intention. Salt in water is an added cleanser. If you do not have these readily available, and you feel affected by the energies of others in a way that has drained you or tainted your energy, stand under the shower and intend that the water cleanses your energies. Also, if you can buy epsom salts, you can add some to your bath.

Standing in wind, especially by the sea, purifies the energies. Activities, such as sailing, jogging, picnicking, walking, and exploring along windy coasts assist cleansing. Also, simply walking through a forest or park is extremely cleansing. You can assist cleansing by visualizing the branches of trees, leaves, and flowers washing your energetic bodies as you walk.

Keep your dwelling and where you spend much of your time clear. If you live in a dust-filled, messy place, it will be hard to keep your own energies clear. Regularly, air the home and where you spend your time. You can burn natural incense. Enable a lot of natural light to brighten your living space. Playing uplifting music, especially spiritual, also helps clear.

Successful people remove things in their lives that are not working for them. Purifying yourself of all that holds you back from being your best self is essential. Be aware of when your energies need to be cleared. Don't wait to clear when you just had an argument. Clear each time you feel you have been affected, but once you have had time to process your feelings. Clear regularly. Identify habits that are not good for your well-being. Take one at a time and choose appropriate strategies or elemental forces to remove them.

When you purge and purify, you clear space for other and higher energies to flow into your environment and life. It is universal law that all vacuums created must be filled. Life includes tough times. Embrace your trials with knowledge that even though they can be immensely painful, they will bring in the good. Clear so the good ushers in. This is key to bringing these higher frequencies and forms into your life.

> *"For a seed to achieve its greatest expressions, it must come completely undone. Its shell cracks, its insides come out and everything changes. To someone who does not understand growth, it would look like complete destruction." (Cynthia Occelli)*

## Additional Message for Your Key To Success

It is now time to undergo purification. You must
clear old habits, patterns and debris. To move
onto embracing even more abundance and
light. Set a time for you to go out into
nature. In nature, start your ritual of
cleansing your mind—say, "I intend to
fill my mind of all that does serve my
highest goals." Cleanse your heart—
Say, "I intend pure love."
Your body—"I intend
its utmost care."
Your spirit—"I intend its
expression." Allow the
breeze, sun, and sweet
aromas to cleanse
all that blocked
these.

~

## ⇐ 7 ⇒

# Key #7: Developing Your Whole Self

*The universe is moving towards wholeness no matter what you
do. We need to access and bring our spiritual intelligence into
our daily activities with the objective of bringing the spiritual,
mental, emotional, and physical bodies in balance and bringing
our fragmented aspects of those into harmony.*

## Introduction

All of creation is purposeful. Each element of creation
is purposefully designed to move towards wholeness and
unity. Each one of us has the same imperative. Grasping
the yearning and call of this universal pull is grasping a
precious key to this alignment—that of developing your
whole self. When you grow in wholeness, you are fulfilling this imperative.

Under the universal law of wholeness, it is understood then that when you move in the direction of separation, isolation, and fragmentation, you are resisting an
imperative for a larger all-encompassing, pulsating, and
expanding universal system. The universe is moving
towards wholeness no matter what you do. Yet, within
the concept of wholeness is free choice. Without grasping
and using this key, we tend to have less real success in life

because we are operating within a materially based intelligence in calculating and weighing the worth of goals and outcomes. We define them according to false criteria of success, criteria that in fact hinder growth into wholeness and balance.

To truly succeed, we need to access and bring our spiritual intelligence into our daily activities with the objective of bringing the spiritual, mental, emotional, and physical bodies in balance and bringing our fragmented aspects of those into harmony. This is not a philosophical exercise. This has tangible and significant consequences. This demands training ourselves in the art of discipline and submission. When we aim to create balance and wholeness within our own being, we become the physically present catalyst for change in our own lives, families, communities, and planet.

## Integrating All Aspects of Self

Developing our whole selves starts with the integration of all of our fragmented parts. It does not work to be an activist out there screaming about oppressive systems or even at home blaming your partner for your relationship troubles if you are not whole yourself. You just cannot expect the world around you to fall into any notion of order or rightness if you yourself are fragmented.

Success in your life is going to depend on your own integration of self into balance. Change is happening anyway, but positive change is going to depend on humanity's growth into wholeness. Therefore, you need to take disciplined action to apply wholeness in your life. You need to use the key of spiritual awareness of purpose. It affects everything. In absolutely everything, from the personal to the political, success rests on your ability as a spiritual activist to contribute your wholeness.

Integration towards wholeness does not in any way mean that you forfeit your uniqueness. As a female, you do not succeed in the long run by eliminating your feminine self to take on male attributes in the workplace. As a person of a particular faith, neither does understanding the other and finding common ground mean needing to give up your religion. As a boss in a company who has a responsibility to lead, you will ensure failure if you relinquish power for the sake of the idea of non-hierarchy and egalitarianism. This is wrong understanding and action.

To become whole and be a catalyst for wholeness, first you embrace all your aspects. This means even your "bad" parts. You embrace your shadows, weaknesses, faults, guilt, worries, pain, and bad habits. Those aspects that no longer work for you may be released after you acknowledge and accept them as part of your existence. Purge and purify, which is in itself a step-by-step, layer-by-layer process. They do not go away by ignoring or denying them. That is not the right method for creating balance. Leaving parts out because you don't like them or others have punished you for expressing them leaves you fragmented and stunted with regard to who you are and who you are becoming.

*Integration of a Whole Contributes to a Greater Whole*

When you stand in your own unique attributes, as imperfect as many will be, you are on your path to purposefulness. Your acceptance of all parts and the integration of them contributes to an even greater wholeness. You, the tools you use (i.e. identities), and those other forms you strive to embody all form the building blocks for greater things.

There are many ways you contribute to a greater whole. So, if you are in an organization and male, embrace your aspects of being a male. These might mean you are contributing in a way that gives people needed direction, focus, and discipline, among so many qualities that are masculine in essence. If you are a female, hold onto and, in fact, develop your feminine attributes because you are likely uniquely gifted with more of that essence that a workplace or organization needs for success (especially regarding things like teamwork, networking, and diplomacy).

The world's religions and faiths have such an important role to play in creating wholeness and peace. On one level, it is true that religions have played a pivotal role in our history in creating some of the most violent wars. On the most fundamental level, it has always been individuals who are fragmented themselves and sought oneness with others by, conversely, dividing themselves from others—an inevitable expression of a fragmented self. During a recent visit to Georgetown University, Maryland, a theologian active in interfaith dialogue exclaimed to me how unfortunate it is that there is such a misunderstanding of the purpose of interfaith initiatives. The purpose is to express the uniqueness of each religion. Only through the embrace of each person's individual faith can a real dialogue about purpose and direction for common understanding and collaboration be achieved.

Yet, I have to point out that while this is a breakthrough, it cannot contribute much in the way of true understanding and collaboration. Firstly, if what we mean by religion is the choosing of directives that were for a specific place, time, and context that applied today can only contribute to division, then that is moving against wholeness and integration. That is still operating at the intelligence levels of analytical thinking and legal analogy, which can be useful, but certainly not with blindness to Divine purpose. That is running the risk of being shut down from spiritual intelligence while being ignorant and oblivious to the role we play as the building blocks for something larger than ourselves.

Religion is an expression of you. It is not you. Therefore, to ensure your expressions are those of your most authentic principled self, you must work on your own integration of self, first. If we ourselves are fragmented individuals at the table doing the dialoguing and neglecting our own personal fixing, world peace will continue to be a fantasy.

Basic biology and even man-made social structures illustrate how interdependent and functionally purposeful these wholes are. Just as the cell makes up our organs, our organs function perfectly together to support the functioning of ourselves as the organism. Those organizations contribute to our communities and perhaps countries—albeit, both negatively and positively. Yet, these countries are interdependent supranationally. A hierarchal differentiation exists as a means for integration of all dynamic parts ultimately for larger purposes. If one part is dysfunctional then the larger system it supports will tend to be dysfunctional.

## Prioritizing Soul Growth

If we are to succeed at the various goals and creations we dream, we need to develop ourselves, as the basic building block and dynamic within the larger wholes. Therefore, developing your whole self requires starting on a much more fundamental level of being within our system of self. The most fundamental is that of the soul. Once we orient ourselves to the growth of the soul, we are successful in all we do.

If you are not sure what to study—as happens nowadays with many young people—yet, you enroll in university, you might find yourself meandering through college. You are trying this subject and that one. Along the way you get a taste of what moves you and what bores you. There is nothing seriously wrong with this except for the fact that you took the long way around. Perhaps all these different experiences will be integrated to form something unique and that was your path for your highest potential for expression. This meandering indicates to me that more young people are taking the search for meaning seriously. Yet, in many cases we waste precious time.

Very often wasting time and the mistakes made along the way of unconsciously finding our self has significant consequences. Meandering is not always a benign undertaking. It can have dire consequences to others and ourselves. We need to make our soul evolution a priority. Thereafter, choices are made with much simpler calculations. They simply need to be aligned with and submitted to our priority. Life's complexity is reduced.

Not only do we make life simpler, we realize how much help we have along the way. When we set our sights on the ultimate purpose, that is, the fulfillment of soul expansion, as a cumulative project, we set in motion opportunities to give our growth direction. The universe aligns behind you in what you are focusing on. Therefore, you want to be guided all the way up to the highest possibilities, to stretch yourself to reaching your highest potentials. You do this by choosing soul purpose, its wholeness and growth.

When you prioritize your soul as the system from which you wish to operate in this world, you allow the ability to access soul wisdom, your spiritual intelligence. With spiritual intelligence you guide yourself to the right people and situations. God and the universe are always on your side, guiding you. When you listen to guidance, you stop at what you are guided to take notice of and allow yourself to see higher meaning and purpose. You learn to do this by making your soul a present part of your being and therefore choices and actions.

You are not atomistic as a physical self with a brain. Your whole self includes your emotional, mental, spiritual, and physical bodies. Embracing each aspect makes you aware of how they function independently and interdependently. You tune in better to your emotions, knowing full well how it is going to impact your mental state eventually. You tune into your mental state because you know that through *dis-ease*, it is going to eventually cause disease in your body. By being aware of how all these dynamic parts of you affect the other parts, you are probably not going to neglect them. You make developing and integrating them a choice as part of your whole concept of self. You make better decisions as to what is in alignment with your soul growth and what detracts from it.

## Steps to Develop Your Whole Self

Soul growth is a principle, and therefore the guiding strategy and means to utilizing your key; all other strategies then become easier to use once soul growth is prioritized. There are steps to enabling your soul growth and developing your whole self. To develop your whole self, seek meaning in situations you face. If situations and people repeat themselves, they are offering something to you so that you recognize it. Integrate what the world is mirroring to you as a part of your spiritually aware path to success. They are showing facets within you. These could be our shadow parts or negative traits. You are being asked through such an exercise to integrate a higher perception of them to decide how to work through them. Choose how you will purify and let go of those that are not working for you or in fact hindering you from focusing on developing yourself.

Our soul requires the most attention; yet, the above are often the most neglected. When we are disconnected from our highest sense of self and the guidance it brings, we can seriously lose direction. To be most successful with this life, we should strive to learn as quickly as possible from all life lessons, resolve to integrate these lessons for ever better fulfillment of purpose, and use all spiritual resources to guide ourselves to get there. The means to do this is connection and continual renewal of connection.

How does your physical body serve you? Often people are working so hard that they neglect the vehicle in which Source placed the soul to fulfill its objective. Ease out of the habits that are ruining your physical health. Include simple habits, such as getting sufficient sleep, eating wholesome nutritious food and working in up to half an hour of exercise five times a week. Your body has a sacred purpose.

If you are tired, irritable, easily upset, run-down, and exhausted, how are you going to raise up your energies? If you are stressed all the time, how can you enjoy life or the good things you have? You will likely bring others down, not up. You will overlook so many opportunities your guidance is presenting to you if you are not centered in emotional balance. Spend more time with family and loved ones. Take a long bath, a long walk in nature, a jog; laugh more, meditate or pray. Tend to your emotional well-being because its balance is critical to overall health, well-being, and your ability to function wholly.

A tired, emotionally strained person will have a hard time maintaining mental alertness and sharpness. You need to be mentally awake and clear to make sound decisions and act throughout your day with the best of actions. The emotional and mental bodies are closely tied. The physical body has a direct impact on mental abilities; so keep the mind sharp with exercise, food rich in vitamins, and enough sleep. Take training courses and narrow your learning endeavors to serve your soul purpose. Be selective. You can't do everything. Choose what is in alignment with your highest objectives.

Developing your whole self is all about gaining awareness of how all parts of your being work together towards wholeness and supporting the process. As the organism you are, each cell, organ, and the emotional, mental, physical, and spiritual bodies are working to support you. You are in the driver's seat. You have responsibility to ensure that your organism is optimally fulfilling its universal purpose. By working towards completeness and unity by submitting to the Higher will of God, you are reaping the experience of success the fastest way.

*"To submit isn't to be forced. It is to yield to a force greater than your own, in order to become part of the whole." (Dianna Hardy)*

### Additional Message for Your Key to Success

Choose a current situation. Be an observer of it.
You do this by taking a perspective that does not
entertain any extremes of the situation. If you are
considering any major changes, take a step
back. There is an aspect to that one thing
that you can include. Add it now to form a
more balanced and integrated perspective.
Open yourself even further to the wisdom
and guidance of your soul. Ask how you
can integrate this perspective to support
a higher and more balanced way of
acting. Choose alignment with your
soul purpose and reflect. Your
criteria include seeking
balance on your
path to Source.

～

## ⪻ 8 ⪼

# Key #8: Beliefs of the Mind

*Our beliefs and thoughts form our perspective or approach to life. This belief will be seen in one's behaviour; through repetition our behaviour creates our experience; that experience will create our reality.*

## Introduction

Our beliefs critically determine our success in life. Have you noticed how one person's pessimism seems to overshadow things that an optimist would have noticed right away and honed in on as good? These two people will have vastly different experiences in life. The pessimist fails to embrace the good and the optimist does not allow the downs in life to keep her from moving forward. She does not fear falling, so takes the chances at success because when she falls she is back up running toward her goal again. Beliefs are a key ingredient to how we prepare and orient ourselves for success or failure.

Our beliefs and thoughts form our perspective or approach to life. This belief will be seen in one's behaviour; through repetition our behaviour creates our experience; that experience will create our reality. No matter what demeanour you present to others or words you may utter, the world will be a mirror of your inner state formed by thoughts and beliefs. That is why our beliefs are a powerful source for creating the realities manifested outside of ourselves.

### The Unconscious Mind and Affirmations

We ought to begin our reorientation to life by asking what thoughts and beliefs it is mirroring within us. Things we keep replaying in our minds become central in our consciousness. Beliefs about the world and ourselves have reached us at the core level because we are programmed to think about life a certain way by a society that relentlessly pursues this agenda, cementing the thoughts into our minds. Not only do these thoughts manifest in our environment, they determine how we experience life. In essence, many feelings of powerlessness or strength, unhappiness or joy are determined by how we are processing information we receive about the world around us and are saving it in our minds.

Changing our experience starts with changing the dialogue in our minds. We can shift our thoughts through affirming what we want in our experience. Affirmations for positive thinking are thoughts that when used correctly and consistently produce noticeable effects in how we change our orientation towards life. When we shift our thoughts, we can more easily change our actions. Our experiences shift and life can be much more joyous and abundant. We face life lessons and trials and accomplish things with greater ease.

Through affirmations we program the mind much like a computer because our unconscious is like a computer system. It is something we do on a constant basis.

We can be affirming that we do not want commitment, peace with colleagues, or a raise and we can be affirming that we want other things in our lives. Because this occurs at a deep unconscious level, we are often unaware that we are making these statements that inevitably guide our actions. Often we are telling ourselves the opposite of what we really want on a conscious level.

How might a pessimist be a pessimist, or a forward looking person have gained such an attitude, you might ask. There are many factors. However, take, for example, a teenager who is repeatedly told by her mother, "You are so lazy; your room's always a mess!" She will be programmed by her well-meaning mother actually *not* to clean up and rather to view herself as incapable of being able to do simple tasks such as tidying after herself. Her programming, however, affects not only her ability to tidy her room but to engage in other activities. Whether we are affirming attitudes from others or ourselves, that serve us or not, we are always engaging in an incredibly powerful resource. The key is to tap into and use this source of power for our highest good.

*How to Use Affirmations and Visualization*

As Albert Einstein said, "Your imagination is your preview of life's coming attractions." Affirm what you want to see manifested, what it is you want to be, or who you want to be. Repeat a simple and short affirmation several times throughout the day, over several days. It is best to write it down and place it where you will see it often. Bit by bit the message goes deeper into your being. You can do this while doing visualization so that the words anchor more easily into your unconscious.

There are numerous studies on the power of visualization. Express your words while visualizing yourself being the kind of person you want to be, or enjoying the experience you desire. I studied visualization techniques at university and used them from a younger age in sports at the behest of my coach. One simply sees herself doing the activity over and over every day affirming the ability. The muscles respond to the brain impulses and are honed through visual practice.

A sports coach who coached some of the top football (soccer) teams in England explained to me once how successful she was using visualization together with affirmations. Because athletes are all pretty much at the same physical abilities and skills at the premier league, what differentiates the players from one another is their beliefs. She told how she emptied their minds of all their negative and self-defeating attitudes. Then she drilled into them affirmations. She succeeded in helping bring the worst team in the league (at the time) to first place.

Make sure your affirmations contain only positive words. The unconscious mind has difficulty computing negatives. It will simply delete them during downloading. For example, if you are affirming that you do not want to have a fight with your boss, you are actually computing within your unconscious, "I want to have a fight with my boss," because the "not" is disregarded. You are focusing on what you do not want rather than placing a picture in your mind of what you *do* want. You are producing the very thing you do not want to materialize.

Emotions play a pivotal role in affirmations. If you are affirming that you do not want to have a fight with your boss, yet you feel dread and fear each time you affirm this, you are adding to the mix a potent ingredient, brought into your physical environment through your feelings you affirm, in this case a fight. As a result, it is essential that you feel the *positive* sensations in your body that accompany your *positive* phrasing. Say, rather, "I feel peace around Joe (boss)," and really feel what it is like to be in that room with him and remain calm.

If when you are saying the affirmations you are countering them with negative beliefs, for instance, "I really cannot see myself feeling peace around Joe, impossible!" then you are defeating the purpose of the exercise completely. In such a case, embrace that the process may take longer because you will have to start with smaller steps that your mind can accept with some effort. In this example, you may want to ask yourself, first of all, "What am I really afraid of?" "What is the worst that can happen? Use affirmations that build on each other in order to take small steps in the direction you want to go. In this instance, you could then proceed to say, "Joe and I are now coming to a better understanding," acknowledging that a process is in place. When you feel you are ready to move forward, you could then say, "Joe and I are now getting along," and then, "I feel peace around Joe."

When visualizing and affirming, do so either in the present or past tense. If you keep seeing and saying that you will do something or be the person you want to be, that vision becomes illusive. It remains an abstract idea that you tell your mind to continually pursue. In other words, it will remain unattainable because it remains in the future. An affirmation is the act of affirming that something is or that something has been accomplished.

Affirmation and visualization are powerful resources for achieving what you want in your life and the higher essence you want to let shine through you. Because laws of the universe are exact, your environment must start shifting when you have anchored changed thought patterns into your unconscious. Below are some affirmations that evoke a particular modality of power to get started with. Depending on what you wish to work on first, choose only one, write it down and place it in spaces you will see it, i.e. mirror, pillow, purse, car dashboard, folder, etc. Use it for at least a week.

> *"What we are today comes from our thoughts yesterday, and our present thoughts build our life of tomorrow: Our life is the creation of our mind." (Buddha)*

### Additional Message for Your Key To Success

*Affirmations to Use*
I use my feelings for the right actions.
I am responsible for my life's direction and I choose (_____).
I am successful at (_____).
I love myself unconditionally.

∾

## ≈ 9 ≈

# Key #9: The Law of Love

*When your work becomes a product of your own unique passion and essence of love, you have successfully accessed the highest and most powerful vibration of the universe. You are working with God.*

## Introduction

Love is our essence, from which we were made, and to which we thus yearn to return. Because of the act of love and passion, your parents produced you. Not just us, every act of creation happens with love. Herein lies one of the most precious keys for your path to success. Nothing you dream of, of the highest essence, can manifest without the energy of love. Giving from the energy of your passion will produce the side effect of success. When your work becomes a product of your own unique passion and essence of love, you have successfully accessed the highest and most powerful vibration of the universe. You are working with God.

## What Love Can Do

Being the supreme form of light frequency, love can break down barriers within the hearts of loved ones and the walls put up by enemies. How is it couples still get married and wholeheartedly make their vows despite the odds of marriages lasting these days? Have you ever wondered how two groups whose histories are marred in tribal or ethnic killing and war can produce children who today call themselves one nation? These acts defy pure logic.

Love is the most potent source of power, yet least understood in all disciplines and practices—again, individual and family therapy, strategic management, studies for diplomacy and international relations, and even religious sermons. Without harnessing the law of love, you will have difficulty achieving true success, whatever the area of life. To effectively deal with our personal problems, anxieties, phobias, addictions, and personality flaws love is central. Your success is squarely dependent on this key no matter what level you are working at. By working with Source power and flowing with the laws of love, you give yourself the ability to create heaven on earth.

Love can potently transform situations and create change. When you direct the energy to any situation or person, you are automatically and spontaneously enabling a transition to a higher form of it or expression from within it. This is the meaning of empowerment.

Politicians and economists determining much of the way the world is functioning today are exercising a false sense of success based on the power of might. Political scientists are often so shaped by shallow ideas deemed to be objective truths; they cannot help but pass misdirected understandings of power onto generations. When love dispels hate and apathy, it is not passive as it produces consequences. Love as a core part of spiritual activism can ultimately bring about a whole new reality of peace. Love is not only political; it is the most powerful force and act.

Love heals and sustains us in the darkest hour. My father was amongst several hundred thousand German children put in the Oxbüll Lager (camp) in Denmark toward the end of the second World War and was among a small percentage to survive. I grew up with him reminiscing all the time about the indispensible power of his mother's love and her many acts of sacrifice during the harshest two years of his life, when he ate no more than the other children, most of whom died of hunger or disease. In fact, he was placed in a room to die and was the only child known in that area of the large camp to make it out. He attests his strength came from being nurtured so selflessly.

*Love is the Act of Giving*

Love entails action. Love is not just a feeling, as opposed to what we falsely presume. Where there is conflict between people, the road to peace can never begin with *feelings* of love. It does not work that way. It may begin with a feeling of hate that when embraced creates pathways to the love buried beneath pent up emotions. But, whether a lack of love exists or whether the energy of hate is most present, the action begins with a deed. True love can never be faked, but it becomes manifested through a deed of deciding to choose love. Consequences of a deed of love include creating the feeling of love, and eventually the *experience* of love.

True success is through doing what it takes to love. There are many things in life we would rather not do and rather not deal with. When we have marital problems, problems with siblings, parents, children or friends, how many of us really have made the decision to do this deed as a verb when we are feeling low, maybe loathed, after we have exchanged too many nasty words, after things seem to have gone too far too long ago? Worse, how many of us *feel* like looking within ourselves for clues to our part in creating our failed situations? Few. Think of all the relationships some of us let ride to the end because we were either self-indulgently righteous or too lazy to put in anymore effort. True success comes about through a spiritual growth through cracking open our hearts, embracing our darkness, taking responsibility, and letting out light to heal ourselves and heal others. This is the process of freeing ourselves from the barriers to our own love that is the key to growth and success.

The law of love states that you experience love by giving love. You have love in your life when you give it freely, when there are no strings attached, and when you continue to love even when you do not see love returned to you. But it will return to you, if not from the person you are giving love to, from someone else. Bottom line, you must receive what you give. If you want love, give love!

The great religions implore us to: "Love your neighbour as you love yourself" (Saint Paul, Galatians 5:14). It is possible to do. I know of a woman, Hadia El-Attar, who thought she had a bad relationship with her neighbour because when she greeted her the first few times the neighbour simply looked down or looked the other way. Hadia made a choice to continue her simple expression of love. Hadia saw her neighbour virtually every morning as the two stepped out to head to work and every single morning Hadia mustered the courage to say a pleasant "good morning" greeting. For a whole year, Hadia persisted in loving her neighbour. After a year to the same month, one morning the woman suddenly stopped upon Hadia's greeting and burst out in tears. Hadia told me the shaking woman raised her eyes for the very first time. She told Hadia that Hadia was the only friend she had, and that the next day she was going to be admitted into a psychiatric hospital. She profusely thanked Hadia for being her friend.

Not only are such approaches to treating other people with love and dignity possible, they work to empower others and transform relationships. With persistence and continuous effort, changes must happen and hearts melt. Usually the reasons for seemingly unloving behaviour towards us have nothing to do with us directly. It is not personal although it is there to teach us to love more deeply. Sometimes we are at fault and need to learn to love more deeply, too. Just as importantly, from this example, we can understand also how the law of harvest works. When you give and give and let nothing stop you from giving, the seed you planted and watered consistently with love must sprout! It may take a long time. We cannot see the roots growing. But, one day, and often it is sudden, a change will happen in your life. The law is precise.

Success at transforming any situation requires that you keep your focus on the act of giving, and relinquish the ego's desire to see quick changes. If you prioritize giving for any other reason—even for the person and even for the sake of peace—your expectations will be dashed, because you will be tested in intentions and patience. We forget that we are here to be tested in deeds and we are here within perfect timing to give uniquely the love that is meant to flow through us. Yes, we are meant to enjoy the creations and blessings of love and it is our right to, but we are gifts gifted to this earth. To give love is an imperative.

Love is the most simple and basic part of our experience on this earth and therefore the basis from which all our actions should be aligned. If our deeds are in alignment with love, we have absolutely nothing to worry about. Success will not elude us. If we are living love and giving love, surely all our deeds will be blessed, must produce fruit, somewhere and somehow, and experience the highest form of success.

*Working with the Law of Love*

There are numerous ways you can create potent forms of success. You will fail at each try, however, if you do not start with yourself. Find ways to gift yourself with love today: relax, even if you have no time to, take a walk in nature, take a long bath with candlelight, indulge in something healing. Take a moment when you are ready and forgive yourself for past things you simply can no longer change because you cannot give love if your own energies are blocked by any form of unwillingness to receive love. You have much to do and accomplish, so move on with what you have learned and can now offer.

Forgiveness is a powerful way of extending love. When you feel ready, give love to those who have harmed you, too. Being ready will require making that choice. In her poem, "The Uses of Sorrow," Mary Oliver tells, "Someone I loved once gave me a box full of darkness. It took me years to understand that this, too, was a gift."

The greatest gift is to ourselves because when we forgive we release the pain that is held in our own hearts, poisoning no one else's but our own bodies. And, in each test and in each calamity that we meet in this life, therein is a lesson to learn and from which to grow. In each test, we find an opportunity to purify. In each test, we have an opportunity to act in the best of ways and continue to give love no matter what, and when we do this from and for the Divine, we are alchemized.

Each morning when you wake up, make a number of intentions to give love! Praise and worship is giving love. To experience and feel a life of success, giving must be your goal each and every day. Ask yourself, to whom can I give and what can I give? Touching another is giving love. Make sure to hug your family with the firmest embrace. Patience with whoever stretches it for you is giving love. Instead of barking at the kids to hurry through their breakfast, speak gentle words. One's true character is primed for success within the home where the world cannot observe you. There are endless ways you can use your time today to give love. Every day you open your eyes, make love a choice and you will reap true success.

*"It's not how much we give but how much love we put into giving." (Mother Teresa)*

### Additional Message for Your Key to Success

Love transforms and transits all other forms of
energy. Resolve today to feel love for yourself,
live love, be love and give love, and
your success is manifesting in all you
intend with love.

~

## ᕗ 10 ᕘ

# Key #10: Intention for Manifestation

*Intention for manifesting something is setting clear in your mind what you want, where you want to be, who you want to be, and what you want to see materialize. Intention is more than focus because it sets energies in motion.*

## Introduction

To manifest changes in life and changes in the world, some of us start out full throttle with energy but then the ball of fire we have mustered eventually crashes. This is actually a means for failure. You might be able to recall great ideas for projects that have simply been put aside. Love energy is potent energy that requires direction in order to materialize according to laws that govern manifestation. Entrepreneurs like to call this focus. It is actually more than that. To manifest dreams requires that you work with the keys of intention and manifestation.

### Making Clear Intentions

Intention for manifesting something is setting clear in your mind what you want, where you want to be, who you want to be, and what you want to see materialize.

Intention sets energies in motion. In my experience and according to the laws governing intention, once an intention has been firmly made and actions are aligned, a cumulative effect eventually appears, often even suddenly. After creating that impetus in the early phase, through a lot of dedication and discipline, the universe then helps make everything fall into place from sources and in ways we usually least expect.

Making a clear intention serves to direct the energy. There are strategies to ensure you set your intention correctly. To transit the energy of hoping, ask yourself, what could I possibly fear? If your mind comes up with answers, explore them. Do not stick them to the back of your mind or deny them. Embrace those shadows. Pull them out into the light so they are in full view. Logically analyze where they originated from, what role they have played in your life so far, even thank them for surfacing from your unconscious, and tell them they may leave now because you no longer fear them. Deal with them like they are real, because at some level you made them real, so they are there.

If you do not work through them, they remain buried, waiting to express themselves at the first opportunity. If you know you want something but your attention and focus is divided among possibilities or something is telling you that you cannot have what you want, you allow your goal to be unattainable. This way, your goal rides on mere hope. Let these shadows no longer play messages in your unconscious. You must have your goal in full view. You must breathe your goal so that your thoughts follow it clearly on autopilot and know no other way.

Ensure that you are consciously formulating and executing intentions that are in alignment with your heart's desire and the highest good. Second, consistently check or audit that your thoughts are positive and that you consciously choose to stand for what is right and just. Third, if not, change those thoughts by choosing those that serve your highest goals. What you affirm, embody through repetition, do as learned behaviour, or believe becomes programmed within the unconscious. The mind also tends to fall to the ego's promptings as it wanders to the negative. Your programmed mind is wired to assist you in executing what it is programmed to do, whether doing good or doing harm. The unconscious does not differentiate. And, your programmed mind must manifest. That is law. Deep beliefs set forth with emotion form an even stronger magnet to manifestation than the conscious.

Before anything became part of our material existence, it was first there in the mind. Similarly, we go about building a house first by dreaming about what we want it to look like. Then we put together an outline or blueprint. Metaphorically speaking, some of us do erect houses without such a plan. When we do, we often end up with a different house than what we envisioned or wanted; often it is very unstable, and usually short-lived.

If you do not make clear intentions to take the path that is best, to take the higher road, and in so doing manifest what you truly want and what brings joy, your unconscious with its usual way of operating will do the steering for you. In order to break away from past modes of thinking and practices upon which your current behaviours and choices are being directed, you must set new intentions. When you make an intention, you change the course of your life.

Crucially, before you make your intention, ask yourself why you want what you are pursuing. What kind of person will it make you? Who will you be when you picture yourself with what you want? Above all, ask if it takes you closer to your purpose or further away from it. Make sure that what you want is in alignment with your soul growth, enables you to express yourself, and serves you and all concerned within what is good for all and harms none. Ask that what you are pursuing be within Divine order. Being in a calm, fasting, or a meditative state helps you align your intention with your soul purpose. Intentions are powerful and hence should be given time for reflection and clarity.

*Working with Intention*

Intentions can take on many forms. Always write your intention down on paper. You can then make your intention through prayer, affirmation, or visualization. You may want to dedicate a good few hours to sit quietly in a field, the forest, or other place and be with nature, and simply state your intention out loud for all nature to hear. You may opt to sit with a loved one and make the intention in front of him or her. What is important is that you express it to the universe in some way.

Once you make an intention, know that it is in existence on the spiritual plain. It is setting in motion what is required for the universe to align behind where it is aimed. God, His angels, and the universe will facilitate your choice for a higher way. Your only job is to continue thinking in this new way so that your unconscious absorbs your new direction as its new mantra. Make a decision to stand by your choice. Make a decision to discipline yourself to follow this choice in not only your beliefs, but also your actions.

Disciplining the Self means to repeat affirmations and behaviours until they are your breath. Remind yourself everyday of your intention by seeing what you are manifesting. For example, if you want a larger house ask that it serves your ultimate purposes. Affirm your new home with gratitude and love. Find a picture of a dream home and put it on your desktop. See it every day. Look at the furniture you need for your new home, and start matching. Resonate with the frequency of your home and how it serves your mission for expressing yourself better.

If you want to take time off to relax and enjoy some peace but feel strapped for money, make the intention. Afterwards, similarly place pictures of the place you want to visit somewhere you will look several times a day, such as on the fridge. Sit quietly every day and imagine that you are in this place. Visualize: sink your feet in the sand, dip your toes in the water, sit back and feel the warm sun on your skin, smell the sweet perfume of flowers and trees that the breeze brings you. Strategize: flip through adverts, such as last minute deals, and put aside savings.

If you want, for example, better relationships or people to enter your life, intend it! You will want to manifest those people and the lessons they offer you in your life journey because we grow profoundly through the love, support, and life lessons—gifts they are meant to bring us and vice versa. Then materialize this goal and purpose by reading out loud the intention you wrote on paper every morning as a mission statement. Put details onto the paper—list exactly what you want to manifest and how you feel doing so. *Believe* the situation already exists, *feel* the joy and peace in it. Strategize: take action to now, and every single day, reach your goal.

If you want to see a clean environment, such as after an environmental disaster, intend, such as through prayer, affirmation, or meditation, and then hold the focus. Holding the focus includes visualizing or meditating on the pristine picture you have in your mind of the place, several times a day. Manifesting this picture is more effective if done in groups. Obviously, the birthing of such a vision depends on a collective consciousness, including those who have opposite visions, such as those motivated and steered by greed, anger, etc. Change often takes time and the larger the goal often the longer the gestation period. Simultaneously, take action: lobby appropriate governments and institutional bodies, volunteer with an organization that has strategies already in place, make others aware of what is needed for the situation. These all form the blueprint. Leave the rest to All That Is.

Let no one or anything deflect you from where your intention is already carrying you once you have made it. When you defy what others think is reality, they may try to hold you back because *their* reality is defined by limitations. They may not be jealous or vindictive but simply limited. If someone tells you that your goal is selfish, too grand, out of your league, or impossible, you need not provide justification. Any other consideration is if you are affecting other people's lives by your choice and collectively a compromise is best and serves a larger good, to which your own good is always part and parcel. Not allowing anything to deflect you in no way means you have the right to trample on others' rights or compromise their well-being, and doing so, in fact, will only ensure your "mission" eventually fails. You operate as part of a whole, not as an independent entity. When you work with spiritual keys, however, you will find that you often defy old ways of thinking of your own.

*"Everything in the unconscious seeks outward mani-festation, and the personality too desires to evolve out of its unconscious conditions and to experience itself as a whole."* (Carl Gustav Jung)

### Additional Message for Your Key to Success

You are called to voice what is in your heart.
Your intention must be to let it out for you
to hear it, see it, and acknowledge it. When
you let it out, the universe aligns with its
unique vibration for your unique success.
Write it down. Take it with you out in
nature. With your hand over your heart
and the other over your throat, now feel
it. Say it out loud. Rejoice. You
are now manifesting your
beautiful dream.

~

## ≈ 11 ≈

# Key #11: Prayer

*Prayer is a mercy, as when we return to unveiling the barriers we set up in hearts on the path towards Him and find friendship and guidance when weariness was about to break us, we receive.*

## Introduction

Prayer opens the door to your dreams, ambitions, and heart's desires. Prayer provides the means to triumph over struggles. Even where the dark follows you and you feel the grimness of its grasp, in that is God's purpose so that you hold fast in faith and dedication to the rope or the branch He throws you to pull you to the shimmer of light seemingly off in the distance. The Source of all creation and power has the grandest of plans. In Marianne Williamson's *Illuminata: a Return to Prayer*, she explains that through prayer we access the Source of all power, as "the Lord is Lord of all universes."[14] When you tap into His power, you have the greatest power with you. Prayer is the key to many worlds.

*Benefits of Prayer*

When life squeezes us and we see the truth of our own limited devices, we turn to our Lord to show us why, to show us the way, to give us strength, and to help us in victory. How else could we learn from what our life puts before us but to go through the cycle of pain, denial, disillusionment, searching, surrendering, and opening ourselves to communicating again with our Lord, the Most Merciful, the Most Compassionate. Prayer is a mercy, as when we return to unveiling the barriers we set up in hearts on the path towards Him and find friendship and guidance when weariness was about to break us, we receive.

We receive not only what we want and what is the highest good, but we also tap into our birthright to communicate with our Lord and have access to His power without the need for intervention of any human being. Prayer is the key to taking back our own personal power that we often inadvertently hand over to others. When we communicate openly and fully, we pour out of our hearts the pain, the confusion, and release the disempowerment. In turn, we receive solace, strength, and the wisdom to understand and allow ourselves to be guided. In this process of yearning and submission, we are not just taking the key into our possession, we are using it. We receive the answers we need to change the things we need to, to endure the things we cannot change, and in that is the key to empowerment.

In such Divine connection, we are able to bring heaven on earth. God hears all prayers. Believe, and you will receive. When the Lord, King of all universes, hears us we may even witness miracles. Miracles are proof that we are heard and loved. However, as Maimonides says in *Guide for the Perplexed*, "A miracle cannot prove what is impossible; it is useful only to confirm what is possible." When we do bear witness to and experience the enactment of the law, As Above so Below, in that is a lesson of the immense power we all have within us when we tap into the ultimate power of Source.

*Alignment with Divine Will*

Remember the saying, "Be careful what you wish for because you might just get it?" Be careful what you pray for, too. You may desire something that is not best for you, and you may just get it! When praying for something that you desire, ask that it is for your highest good and the highest outcome for all, and if it is not, ask that it be removed from reach and replaced with that which is better. You may also add that any replacement is something you will be pleased with, too. Then you leave it to God, relinquishing all control for the outcome, because His plan is best.

We have free will and we also co-create with our Divine essence and soul connected to all consciousness. This responsibility results in the variance in pace and depth of our individual and collective growth. When we pray for something we desire, we must prioritize in relation to our growth and our ascension to the Divine.

Not all requests are granted. This is a mercy. Think about the child who asks for an ice-cream and then a chocolate bar and on and on desires to fill her stomach with all the sweets available. She might not quite understand that eating too many sweets will hurt her stomach in the short term and damage her teeth in the long term. As a parent or responsible adult, you would love to make the child smile but know that giving in to such request will cause harm. So, even if the child gets upset you will say, no, and that "no" is an expression of love.

Similarly, God wants what is best for us and often allows the scripting of events to manifest as barriers blocking us from what we want. Sometimes, something else from what we desire will be facilitated that will serve our growth or joy, even if we cannot yet comprehend it. While we co-create and make choices for which we are responsible, there are events that we cannot control. They have been predestined before our souls entered human form. If our prayers seem unanswered, there is wisdom in the silence. Thus, as long as we act with the best of integrity and faith, we can rest assured that what transpires is the highest outcome.

There is a difference between the passion of the heart and the passion of the ego. Rumi reminds us to follow the passion of the heart: "Everyone has been made for some particular work, and the desire for that work has been put in every heart." Passions of the ego can trump the calling of the heart and steer us in wayward directions, just like the reed is swayed to and fro by the wind. This is not to say that the ego cannot serve a purpose in our evolution, as it does. Moreover, we often do achieve what was motivated by the ego. But, in our hearts we feel our true path, the easiest way Home, and from there we can express our unique qualities as a means to following our path.

It is important to ask for help in recognizing what real success is for us so that we can embrace the path to real success and avoid the pain and emptiness of working for the ego. Also, sometimes opportunities pass us by only because we are seeking things that are illusory and not for our greatest welfare. With the aspect of free will we have the ability to do that to ourselves. I know of several people, besides myself, who have, for example, chosen a particular study, career or activity because it was in line with established notions of what is proper: wealth, power, prestige or what is "normal" and therefore success. Those who learn to flow through the guidance of prayer to the right course find their way, which is always much more fulfilling and productive.

If you pray for a partner, a job, a house, or any physical thing but have no guided and larger vision of it or you are looking at titles and signs of outward success, then the universe will offer up indiscriminate potentials along those lines. Clear criteria is abstracted but at the same time refined by guiding values, which are guided by an ultimate vision. We are then in a position of clarity to recognize the fulfillment of prayer when it appears before us and not as easily get sidetracked with illusory successes. Clear criteria entails placing on top of the list a higher or ultimate vision of success that guides in its alignment other or smaller criteria.

### Faith in Praying

Prayer is an act and, as with all acts, will have consequences. However, nothing changes until faith follows the request. Firm faith in God's power to send you what you want as your God-given right is a prerequisite to the fulfillment of His promise, as in Jesus' words, "Ask and ye shall receive." Again, its manifestation sometimes is altered to what we often hold as a narrow vision if it. Sometimes, silence proceeds.

Thus, when we bring clarity in expressing what we want we must also expect that our prayers are answered in its highest manifestation according to a Higher will and knowing of our circumstances, our true path back to our Creator, and all that we cannot know. When we open up to possibilities and expect we are receiving, we must either get exactly what we want or its manifestation in a better, purer, and higher form, even if that is through silence. There are consequences to every request. This is God's promise according to universal law.

We must remember that we are in a world of interconnectedness and change in one area must affect another area. God's bounty is unlimited; however, higher wisdoms include consideration for the whole, not just the individual. This also means that when we are praying for something to change or get better on a level that affects many, our prayers and faith is part of a collective. If there are those praying for the same outcome, such as a war to end, again, success is dependent upon a minimum of those having firm faith taking part in prayer or intention to influence change. For larger scale changes, time is usually of essence.

When we are scattered in our thoughts and feelings, it is hard to pray effectively. Firm faith means that we believe in God's bounty and power and expect our prayers are being answered. When we pray we must do so within a calm grounded state. That way, we feel and activate connection. This does not mean we do not pour out our hearts, as proclaiming our need for His power to work through us enables its flow. However, if we worry, fear, and doubt while asking, we block communication and flow from our end.

Even when silence proceeds, prayer is an act that is of no insignificant consequence. There is no other form of power so great as prayer, as even, or especially, in silence we can receive something so profound—love and peace.

God is love and God is peace. Even through the deepest of pain we have ever encountered, our weary souls are so bathed in love and compassion and our bodies caressed in light, unlike any other experience, by connecting with the Divine. In this silence, we must remember that we are never alone and we will reap sweetness after bitterness, as is universal law.

Prayer has its purpose in granting us our heart's desires for joy and the fulfillment of our life purposes. In this, we must remember to dedicate all that He has bestowed upon us in His way. This way our paths are filled with greater abundance and joy and we fulfill the goals we have promised we would in this life.

*Gratitude*

Prophet Mohammed reminds us, "Gratitude for the abundance you have received is the best insurance that the abundance will continue." Gratitude in prayer also ensures expansion and ascension to the Divine. Hadia, who I spoke of earlier, provides further lessons for reflection here. Hadia's mother, Banan Al-Tantawi was assassinated in Germany when Hadia was only eleven years old in a political assassination aimed to kill both her mother and father, Issam El-Ettar. I spoke to Hadia for at least an hour about various topics, many spiritual, before she imparted the news to me that her 24-year-old daughter had been killed in a car accident three weeks back. I was taken aback by the fact that she did not let me know sooner; then she explained, "When my mother died I said to myself, 'nothing worse in the world could ever happen to me.' Now I know never to say that but to be grateful for all God's trials." Hadia's gratitude embraces calamities even though these may very well bring the greatest forms of pain a little eleven-year-old and a mother could fathom. In that, she will benefit from the law of gratitude in ways we cannot fully comprehend. This life is short and the spiritually evolved know this. Thus, they use the heart to enter the path to greater expansion, not constriction.

Prayer serves constant remembrance of our origin and ignites our longing to its return. When we remember who we are through the waking of our soul's connection to its Source, we are better able to see through the earthly veils of illusion. It is with this orientation, we can set our actions throughout the day in their right course for the highest and most blessed outcomes. We are reminded and given greater opportunity each time we pray to refocus our thoughts, our wishes, and, thereby, our actions, so that we may bring greatest joy and endure the greatest pain. We move closer to our Lord and we hold more love and light within our bodies. Without connection, we miss our path, our purpose; we are powerless. With constant remembrance deep within the soul, we are with the ultimate Source. Being with the ultimate Source, we illuminate our path Home and we illuminate the world.

*Working with Prayer*

There are a few ways you can start using prayer or increasing the use of this key to ensure success in attaining what you want to see changed, your heart's desires, and find the most direct way on your journey home to the Divine. First, thank God for everything; list everything you are grateful for before you retire to bed. Gratitude and praise has the purpose of sweeping in what we are about to receive and multiplying what we already have.

When you wake up in the morning, set your intention through prayer for what you wish to achieve and do throughout the day. That way you align your ego will with the Higher will. Throughout your day link in with God regularly, even if briefly. Set an alarm to do so if need be and take the time to create that line of direct contact. Make prayer a regular part of the your day and you must reap success.

> *"The relationship to one's fellow man is the relationship of prayer; the relationship to oneself is the relationship of striving; it is from prayer that one draws the strength for one's striving." (Franz Kafka)*

### Additional Message for Your Key to Success

A Morning Prayer
Dear Lord, I ask you to come join me, be with
me this entire day. Fill me with your Divine
light, so that it may illuminate my thoughts.
Brighten my ideas, inspire my creativity, guide
me through my tests, bring me to greater
compassion, lead me with wisdom. My
Friend, my Love, walk with me, my family,
my friends who need you most, help all of us
charter our paths with spreading your light
and illuminating where we can in hearts
and in this world. Help me to see your
signs when I turn from your signs. Please
be gentle with me. Please be patient with
me. Pardon my mistakes. Use me, soften
that of me that needs softening.

Strengthen that of me that needs
strengthening and show me how to
align myself to Your will, to Your
love, and be Your love in my life
and in the lives of others. In
Your light, may I walk today.
Thank you.
~ W. Krause

≈

# ≈ 12 ≈

# Key # 12: Faith in the Divine

*As children bring their broken toys*
*With tears for us to mend,*
*I brought my broken dreams to God*
*Because He was my friend*

*But then, instead of leaving Him*
*In peace to work alone,*
*I hung around and tried to help*
*In ways that were my own.*

*At last, I snatched them back and cried,*
*"How can you be so slow?"*
*My child, He said, "What could I do?*
*You never did let go."*

*(author unknown)*

## Introduction

So many of us come to God asking Him to change our circumstances or to give us what we want. When some of us do not see something happen fast, we get angry with God. We plead, we beg and then our actions show we have lost hope in His power. We often behave in all sorts of ways of impatience, ingratitude. The impatient and ungrateful often vow to be people of faith—but then pursue what they want in all sorts of ways, including acting ungodly and downright manipulatively.

Imagine you are pushing a revolving door to try to enter to the other side. At the same time, someone else is pushing from the outside in the opposite direction to enter the building in which you are trying to exit. You push harder because you think the door is stuck or someone is not letting you enter. The push from the other side also increases and so now both of you are pushing with all your might. The door remains where it is because the harder you push the harder the resistance. If you used the key of faith in the Divine and let God orchestrate the events for you, you will be successful. Faith that God's plan is greater and that He will find a way is using the key of faith.

*Faith in Action*

When you act without faith, the other person or thing pushing against us will appear in many manifestations. That is the way we must experience life when we try to push our way through the door without using our key to success—understanding the laws that govern resistance, attachment, and letting go. Sometimes life circumstances become so difficult that people do resign themselves to God's wisdom, knowing, guidance, and power. In any case, though, this resigning of oneself takes work because giving up does not put the key in your hand; disciplined resolve to grasp it does. It is when we take a step in submission to a Higher wisdom that we grasp the key and the door opens for us. All we did was stop resisting what we do not want or try to push our way with our demands and give way to let the Divine do the work.

In intervening in the process, we are usually not just fiercely pursuing something but simultaneously resisting another thing. In essence, we are trying to control that which is also related to perfect Divine will and timing. When we resist something that is not in accordance with our narrow ideals, how we believe our lives should be running, or how quickly our situations should change, that very thing we are resisting, in effect, manifests or, in some way, manifests as great pain. That is what we do when we are breathing life into what we do not want. Instead of focusing on what we *do* want, we have a tendency to give attention and, thereby, energy to the outcome that we fear. In this way, we are interfering with the process of receiving what we want.

What we are set on having may be precisely what we should have and will eventually serve our growth and joy but the fear given to alternative scenarios keeps it in the distance. Sometimes a thing or situation we are desperately holding onto or pursuing is not the best. Sometimes it is decreed that it will be ours but in a different way. Most often we are stopped from having what we believe is best for us because we need to fix something in our lives that is affecting that thing. In that is the lesson and test to trust in the process. In that is the test of our faith in His wisdom. If we do not surrender in faith, we cannot be open to guidance and we remain stuck.

When we are grounded in faith and patience we are truly open to guidance. We can receive guidance when we calm the energies surrounding us so that pathways for connections are intact. We are able to calm the energies when we choose to have faith that we are always assisted and looked after. Faith is ultimately a spiritual and mental choice that the emotions, body, and all energies will synchronize with.

In turn, as soon as we have the connections open and undisturbed, we are capable of spiritually, mentally, and even physically discerning what kinds of things do not feel right, which is best, or what we need to change in our lives to allow what is best to enter. Surrendering enables mechanisms for discernment and perception that may become crucial for choices we will make. It is difficult to make sound life decisions, let alone the decision to choose and follow through consistently with the right actions, when our emotions are flustered and clouded.

*Faith and the Law of Attraction*

How many people have similar circumstances and end up with very different outcomes? Each person, in line with Divine will, creates his own set of circumstances. Sometimes a person places his or her attention on different areas, whether out of fear of a worsening situation or faith that they are assisted and looked after. Other times outcomes are dictated by a set of circumstances that are better and never fully understood.

However, what can always be considered a constant is that firm faith and a focused mind facilitate the path to success. A person who trains his mind to focus assists the process of conscious and unconscious attraction through the matrix of energy to which we are all connected. A person who focuses his attention on what he wants keeps that thing in purview. He keeps his "eye on the ball," so to speak, despite all that may seem to be going wrong.

Like an athlete who keeps calm focus on where he is going, he gives 100 percent to his goal, not 50 percent to its success and 50 percent to its possible failure. As such, he does not resist failure but rather uses all his energy towards his goal. The universe aligns itself behind him when he does not allow himself to be distracted by self-defeating thoughts, and rather thinks and acts with faith in its compassion, mercy, and power.

What many people do not realize is that if they split their attention, they may jeopardize reaching their goal. This is especially the case when the odds are already stacked against them, given the circumstances already in place. The law of attraction is always at work and is directed to anything we focus on at each waking moment.

Your attachment to people or objects places obstacles on the path to achieving what truly brings joy and peace. You know you are attached to something when you are so focused on it that imagining any other scenario or form is impossible for you. Attachment not only suffocates the portals of energy, it forms a frequency around your body that drives away what you desire. Think of relationships you know where the one partner is aloof and barely in touch with feelings, and the other is driven by fear and a desperate need for validation and attention. The energy lines are sullied. Neediness and desperation manifest, too, in one's behaviour. The energy and behaviour such a person exhibits will create an unhealthy dynamic and may cause the other to pull away.

### The Art of Letting Go

There are numerous stories of couples, who wanted to have a child and for some reason could not conceive only to be blessed with a baby once they resigned their will to a higher source. There are many case studies of women conceiving after the couple adopted. Perhaps God's test was for many such couples to increase in their faith. Perhaps their inability to conceive initially was necessary to strengthen their resolve to have a child and cherish the child once received, whether adopted, conceived through medical intervention, or, ultimately, conceived naturally. Although it is an under-researched phenomenon and many "legitimate" causes have been put forward, a spiritual perspective is that the attachment to the form in which the child joins the family is forsaken for a broader view of God's means. Most couples that choose to adopt have accepted the possibility of a higher wisdom. With surrendering we give ourselves permission to step away from trying to control that which we cannot and that which is stopping the flow of abundance into our lives. This one act allows Source to step in.

You are meant to live in peace and enjoy the bounties of creation. However, when you start placing conditions on your ability to be happy, you have missed the meaning of success in life altogether. When you miss the meaning of success, you miss the purpose of tests and forget the fact that you are a custodian of God's gifts. To live a life of peace and contentment you must remember your soul will be tested and tests may involve those things we covet and people we love.

Mary Manin Morrissey reminds us about the universal law of letting go: "The Tao Te Ching says, 'When I let go of what I am, I become what I might be.' When I let go of what I have, I receive what I need. Have you ever struggled to find work or love, only to find them after you have given up? This is the paradox of letting go. Let go, in order to achieve. Letting go is God's law."

Letting go successfully means to understand that you must not end up with the exact thing that you desire. You cannot control things and you definitely cannot control the choices of others. You may be able to influence them. However, letting go means that you accept that what you want or how you think things should turn out may be good but also may not be good.

How do you let go? You rely on the Higher power to open your heart to that possibility and produce the best outcome. This can be done after you have worked in the way of acquiring what you want through the best of actions and integrity, and through discipline and unwavering faith. The rest is opening your heart to let God do His part. Letting go is releasing worry because you are being taken care of and the law of karmic justice is exact.

The spiritually developed person knows that the most important form of success of all is to be the best she can be no matter what the circumstances. Her efforts, thus, are directed to acquiring the development of her soul. If one dirties her soul while pursuing something she desires, then she ends up a deprived soul. If she purifies her soul while pursuing what she wants, then she possesses the greatest gift. It is not what one acquires that defines a person's success or even brings true happiness, but who one becomes while pursuing what it is her heart desires.

In *Mibhar Hal'eninim*, Ibn Gabirol had said, "The height of the intellect is distinguishing between the real and the impossible, and submission to what is beyond one's power." Letting go and letting God is an art. It involves accepting that there is Divine will and that nothing is an accident. In letting go, you are experiencing something, even if nearly unbearable, that is teaching you to surrender. While you learn what it means to surrender, you are accepting that solutions do not lie outside of you but within you. Thus, you strengthen in your abilities to continue to do what is right and mend the flaws within that you need to. Letting go and letting God is far from a passive act.

There are things you can do to surrender and let God do His work. Prayer for help in letting go and gaining perspective will enable you to do so. Affirmations in line with letting go sink into the unconscious, replacing controlling words with thoughts of peace and faith. Use them over the course of your day. Intention made each morning to give over whatever you are dealing with will give you reminders throughout the day to keep your actions in proper alignment. Writing a mission statement with what you desire will set the energies in motion that you need for both support in letting go and success. Below is the Serenity Prayer, which provides the delicate balance of surrender and pursuit.

### Additional Message for Your Key to Success

*The Serenity Prayer*
God, grant us serenity to accept the things we
cannot change, courage to change the
things we can, and wisdom
to know the
difference.

∿

~

# PART TWO

*Stories of **Real** Success*

~

# ⁌ 13 ⁑

# Risk Taking: Pole Dancing and Entrepreneurship

*"I thought I would rather regret having done it and learn from it and give myself the opportunity to grow than to never have done it at all."*

## Introduction

Real success is impossible without taking risks. We need to push our boundaries to grow. We must inevitably feel discomfort when we push these. It can be daunting because beyond the boundaries is the new, the unknown. But what happens when our heart is pulling us to something that is entirely in the unknown or bewildering to parts of family and society? Jane Wilson illustrates how a leap of faith can be taken, indeed, why a leap into the unknown *must* be taken when your heart is guiding you to.

Jane shares her experience of moving from employee to entrepreneur. For her, it wasn't apparent at first that she was pursuing any life purpose or her life's longing. We all have guidance prompting us to embrace our highest expressions. But as she describes, it can be a scary process. There is the possibility that an endeavour will not work out and, for many reasons, not to initiate change. But as she explains, that is never what should stop a person. It does most. Therefore, I share her journey.

Not allowing anything to stop her, she broke traditional notions of success and life goals. As a result, Jane is now living her dream: pole dancing with a philosophy of embracing life that she shares with hundreds of women through her own business.

### Existential Security

Jane tells me, "I grew up in a very safe, rule oriented, highly educated family. So, to succeed in life, you get the best marks, go to the best schools, get the highest academic level that you can and that is going to pave the way to leading a successful life." She describes that the majority of her family went to Queen's University, which is a top tier university in Canada. Her father is an engineer and her family is made up of teachers or those in the commerce industry. She explains, "So, it was school, then a professional career, and the expectation is that you do well at that." What she is describing is precisely the recipe for the type of success that is truly mediocre success whereby one is actually ensured an existential security, but not really living or feeling life.

Jane feels that her path was to go into Early Childhood Education. "I enjoy working with children. And that was tough for my family because it wasn't at a university. It was at a college." Indeed, she was able to choose a different path than her family expected. Yet, Jane worked with top employers, taught at college and so attained one level of success in a competitive world. She adds, "However, I wasn't happy. I knew I wasn't happy but I thought this is the path I am supposed to go on. I became an Early Childhood Educator. I was going to go back and get my Master's because that's the path my family had encouraged me to take, but I wasn't happy while being oblivious that I wasn't happy."

When one is living according to standards that are not one's own and especially not living the highest expression of one's own unique path, there will be signs. For Jane, she shares, "I put a lot of weight on. There wasn't a whole lot of joy in life. You get up, you go to work, you come home, you watch TV. It was a very routine life." But what most people do is ignore that something is not right. They would rather hold onto the known. We justify not peering beyond the comfortable and known boundaries because success is largely defined within the context of security. But then we believe that living the mundane is the right way to conduct our lives.

## Choosing the Unknown

Moving from the mundane into a different place, the unknown, is a choice. We often reach a critical juncture where we are given that opportunity to ask ourselves questions that help us move forward. Jane describes her journey out of this illusion about life and success: "It wasn't until my second child was born and I went back out to work from my maternity leave that I could feel something rumbling." She talks about how she experienced a lot of anxiety before and upon returning to her employer. Essentially, that anxiety was really her guidance telling her clearly that her career choice was not the best. She says, "I went back to my employer; I had a lot of anxiety. I had post-partum depression with both my children. And I just had to question, is this my path for the rest of my life? And if this is the path for the rest of my life, I am going to lead a very boring life."

She acknowledged that "there was this *rumblingness*." But she talks about one day when there was an incident at work and a misunderstanding. She knew she was going to get into trouble and walked into the office and gave her three month resignation. In other words, the universe gave her a nudge in addition to her sense that going back to her employer was not the best for her. The difference between her action on this day and that which most of us take would be the decisive factor for future success. She says, "I didn't have anything else to fall back on or go to but I just felt that I can't keep going down this path." She chose the unknown over existential security.

She explains further, "During those three months, people were telling me I was crazy but I thought 'I will figure it out.'" In fact, her employer told her she would be back. But as she describes, "I came home and turned my house into a childcare centre. So, I brought some children in in the meantime until I could figure it out. And during that time is when I discovered pole dancing."

Often we know long before we grow up what our straightest path is. In Jane's teen years, she was heavily into dance and theatre. She explains, "I loved it. I loved dancing and loved every moment being on the stage. My true path was to be a dancer and choreographer. But I did not know how to make that work. So that is why I went into ECE." She explains further, "So, when I started pole dancing and taking pole dancing classes it started to spark that side of me again, my creative side and re-inspire me to get back into touch with dance."

But here Jane is choosing a path that is not viewed as successful by society. Therefore, in forging forward on her path she had resistance. She describes, "Now it's kind of different because when you think pole dancing you think striptease." And Jane has had her share of questioning about what she was choosing. But she also received support. She informs me that during that time in 2007 there was an underground movement of women taking pole dancing classes. These women would put their videos on YouTube to be able to encourage each other and learn from each other. Already her entrepreneur spirit sensed that this could go further. She tells me, "So, there was a shift coming from the strip clubs coming to the more fitness and gymnastics oriented, Cirque du Soleil type. So it was through them that I started to grasp that this is something that can become more mainstream."

Important to mention, however, is that she illustrates the success of choosing her own way despite fears. She recalls, "I started to lose my weight and I started to take more risks because you get this confidence level that you never had felt before." She was soon hired as an instructor but comments that "Sometimes you just want to run your own race." The journey is not only full of challenges but also real fears. She tells me that, "when the opportunity to purchase the Oakville franchise rights came up that was scary because that means that you are diving right in. You are making that commitment. And when you are running your own business it's all on you. It hinges all on you and your energy."

*Lessons from Diving Into the Unknown*

I ask Jane what experience of success she has gained from this struggle. She explains that, "You can fail but at least you went for it." She adds that "a lot of times I find that people will be presented with the opportunity and they will find every reason not to do it to justify themselves not failing. I haven't failed." Not only did Jane face societal questioning about changing careers to something hardly understood as anything but related to the strip tease world but practical challenges, too. She tells me, "It was a lot of money; I had two little boys. The boys were very small at the time. I needed a full-time income." But none of this stopped her. "I could find every fault in it but instead we dove in and went for it."

But this is a whole journey of successes on a number of fronts. Jane shares, "One of the biggest lessons I have learned is not to hold yourself back. I find that we do tend to hold ourselves back and find a reason not to do something. There are so many reasons not to so we're not putting ourselves out there. I thought I would rather regret having done it and learn from it and give myself the opportunity to grow than to never have done it at all."

However, she confirms that, "Since then I have started a whole new journey." Success unfolds rather into different facets and stages but also into a higher way of perceiving one's path. Jane describes,

> The studio is a lot to run but there is this feeling of self-esteem. We have made the focus of the studio more about taking challenges, taking risks, living life to the fullest. It wasn't on purpose but just shifted that way. At the beginning we were just going to teach women how to pole dance and then it metamorphosed into more than that. It is more about embracing life and diving in, taking the risk and chance and not holding yourself back. That's really what the shift has become in the last two, three years. Now, it's "a life is for the living" approach.

Jane underscores that now she works with clear intention to keep with her business' branding and philosophy. Her philosophy is now primarily to empower women by encouraging them to move past their fears and embrace life. In describing how, Jane recalls that in one example a woman never thought she could perform in front of a group of people. Yet, she wanted the opportunity to put together a performance. When she disclosed her fear about it, Jane and her team helped her choreograph a routine. Jane comments that this woman said it was the most empowering experience she has ever had because it was the first time that she had made an intention for a goal and followed it through until the end.

## Working with Keys to Success

Fulfillment and living life purposefully can be achieved with working with principles to ensure success. When you do, you also know you are on the right path. Jane confirms, "I am 100 percent certain that I am on my life path. There is nothing that gives me any indication that I am not. I believe that everybody has a path that they are on." Importantly, she describes how to work with the keys that help you get to the place of knowing you are on the right path. She tells me, "When you are feeling as though things are not going the way they are supposed to be going, you are frustrated, and you are having all these struggles, to me that's a sign that you are not on the right path." She adds that there are day-to-day struggles, as with anything, but explains, "You know you're on the right path when asking, are the struggles worth it? If you are facing the struggles and you feel they are not worth it then you know you are not on the right path."

Jane works with the keys of success, primarily embracing her purpose, listening to her deeper inner guidance, attuning to energetic vibrations and when needed, shifting thoughts. As she explains, "It's an energy. I have learned so much about energy since opening my own business. The energy, your thoughts, and how you're feeling will completely shape the direction you are going to go on—the thoughts that you feed in, the energy that you allow into yourself and expand into everything. It's a *sourceful* kind of energy." In explaining how to access Source energy, she tells me, "We have our energy we spend throughout the day. But there is a type of energy that is deep down within your core that when you are able to tap into it, for example, when you meditate, and you slow yourself down and you listen to it, that is what will end up guiding you." She affirms how important of a role this key has played for her. She tells me, "I protect that energy. I really listen to it. It's something that I have learned in the past few years how to tap into and use to the best of my abilities."

I prod Jane to tell me what strategies she uses. She describes, "The big one is to slow yourself down, and that's coming from me who doesn't slow down a lot. I have learned a lot about meditation. There are some really great podcasts out there on meditation. That's been very helpful and getting yourself grounded and listening to yourself, and cutting out all the clutter." She laughs, "There are sometimes people in your life that are cluttering your life and just sap your energy. It is just getting rid of the people clutter, the thing clutter, the house clutter—moving things out of your life."

Jane is always full of energy and truly embodies a remarkable zest for life. She is an example for embracing life and living her philosophy she extends to the many women who come through her Aradia Fitness studio. Looking back at her journey, she confirms, "I feel a lot more joy in my life." She had just been chosen to participate in a semi-pro competition for pole dancing, and that is how she feels extremely fulfilled—performing. However, success for Jane and the women who find their expression through her studio is one microcosm of success. Her personal journey is one of embracing something larger, something deeper and therefore meaningful to even the political. It is the microcosm of revering the life we are given by living it and encouraging others to revere theirs. In that is personal and political wisdom to be gained.

~

## ⤍ 14 ⤏

# Curing Cancer When Told It's Over

*"We are people of action. We had to do something about it."*

## Introduction

"At that point, maybe he prayed, but I am not sure he did. Most likely he prayed to die when the doctors told him he had only a few days left." Sunitha Shyam is describing the last days of her father G.V. Shyam Sunder's battle with cancer. I ask to know a little about him. She describes that in her predominantly Brahmin community, everyone was in love with him even though most had never known a Christian. She shares, "If a thief broke into their house, the first person they call is my father. People say his smile is everything. I have never heard him disrespect anyone, the maid, the neighbour, anyone." She can't be exaggerating; her own strikingly beautiful smile is the first thing to hit you. She continues, "My father is the nicest person you could meet—he loves animals. I have seen him save so many animals." I can imagine. I actually witnessed her trying to save stray animals twice, hit by cars, and insist on paying the veterinary bills herself, on those two separate occasions. I ask her about his spiritual practice. Different than what I expected, she tells me, "He did not show people that he prayed, never went to church, but behind closed doors prayed using his heart." Reflecting on his journey to success, she adds, "I believe this all counted."

This is a story of a man from India whose example is extraordinary. He is an example of success not just for those possibly dealing with cancer or a debilitating disease. And let me clarify that in using his example, it is not my intention to present some concoction of a recipe for surviving cancer. He and his wife together now have large numbers of people seeking their support who find themselves in the same predicament of battling cancer. However, his story is one that illustrates the use of a most essential key to success each and every one of us can use when we place all expectation of hope in others and we are let down. I think we all have been there in some form and to varying degrees—through an expert, a teacher, a friend, a caregiver, a parent, a life partner, or a child. We tend to place all hope on charismatic leaders, religious or political, organizations stating a mission we passionately believe in, various establishments, and governments. This is one account of what we do and what is yet possible.

### Playing Cards of a Losing Hand

Sunitha is now going back to that moment when the doctors completely gave up on him. Less than a week is all he was given and he was advised to spend those few precious days with his family at home. She and her family pleaded with the doctors to tell them what they could do to save him, if there was *anything* they could do. She vividly recalls those moments in which the doctors simply refused to discuss anything further: "They told us to just take him home with no intention or provision to follow up." But she is not emotional in her recollection. She is actually smiling while speaking to me in a serene tone of surety and wisdom. She tells me her father wants people to know, to understand.

Imagine being told by your doctor that your life is over in less than a week. Put in Mr. Shyam's shoes, how would you succeed? His is a subjective experience. We are all living our own subjective experience as part of life. Yet, if Mr. Shyam can get through this ordeal, it is possible to get through any ordeal. As a collective, we can learn from the example of him and his family. I attempt to find the essential ingredient for success in such a dynamic. The key is personal power: the taking back of will, resolution, hope and drive and relying on yourself, God—plus all those who don't give up on you.

First, I should acknowledge that the ability to influence the timing of one's death is hotly debated. This is important to address as it has bearing on the meaning of success in our example. There is a long debate on predestination versus individual will. Some say the events of our lives and specifically our time of death is predestined. On the other side of the debate, others say that we have complete free will and we are orchestrators of our own destiny. Here I will also acknowledge that success may be defined by some in such examples as accepting God's will to leave this world, and some hold this understanding irrespective of the debate.

The meaning of success relates directly to the soul's purpose. Success is in aligning the individual will with the Higher will to achieve the soul's purpose. A Higher will may designate that the physical body leaves at a particular time as part of the life journey for the individual. But that was known and agreed to by the individual's soul before beginning that life. Therefore, choosing to prepare to leave this physical world may be in line with a sense of success for a particular individual, who feels an inner knowing that it is time to leave. God knows and the soul, one's inner knowing, knows. No one can claim that that person failed. Otherwise, because life is a precious gift to be used for fulfilling our soul's purposes and our bodies are physiologically designed to protect us with whatever means, it is to be fought for and protected with every ounce of individual will.

Therefore, both predestination and individual will reign. Our soul has a blueprint for our life's objectives: the goals for self-growth we desire to achieve and the creative forms we wish to leave for any of God's creations to enjoy, benefit from and heal through. In terms of soul purpose, the overarching significance is the individual's and universe's evolution. Each one of us must journey back to Source and we are all in this larger plan together. Importantly, people and situations will be part of our life plan for our existence on Earth and will assist us in getting there. They are on that blueprint. There is possibility we miss opportunities or we evade living up to our objectives, or parts of them. So, we certainly can renege on what we came here to do.

Now, what do you do when you are dealt your cards and anyone looking at them would say yours is "not a winning hand"? How will you still reach your objective of winning—at life? I have chosen Mr. Shyam's story to prove that you can still win even with one card left in your hand. After interviewing his daughter, I spoke to two further cancer survivors whose cancer went to stage three. While one altered food habits and the other relied on his and the prayer of others that produced his spontaneous healing and bewildered and shocked the doctors, all shared the experience of making a resolve to take back their power upon their doctors telling them, basically, to look forward to an Afterlife. Somehow what appears to be just as significant is that all had wonderful people around them who did not give up on them no matter what any expert claimed or how right the experts seemed, even when the patients themselves faltered. I hope to live up to Mr. Shyam's wish of having others understand.

*From Bad to Worse*

I ask Sunitha when he suspected he had cancer. "In 2001 he started having numbness in his gums. He went to dentists, different dentists and did various tests on himself," she begins. "No one suspected cancer and not one of us did either. We thought something was wrong about his gum." She tells though that one ENT suggested biopsy. And so, they got tissue from the inner part of his nose. The report came back one week later. Sunitha had a little background knowledge as she was studying zoology in the U.S. at the time. She shares, "I saw carcinoma in the report. Mom didn't know what that meant. So, I told her what it meant. We were in complete shock."

The cancer was found to be located behind the cheekbones. Immediately Mr. Shyam was on radiation in November of that year and went on with it for the next few months. However, the process did not go well. Side effects were already notable. "After radiation finished, his throat was getting constricted," Sunitha says. "These were the side effects. He could not eat much, just mashed up foods. He loves things to be tasty, so he would not eat much. In any case, he did not have an appetite anymore."

As the situation quickly worsened, it is important to note Mr. Shyam's reactions do not suggest a high degree of cooperation or really any form of outward "spiritual" practice. Sunitha describes, "Now, it was getting from bad to worse. My mom would be shouting at him to eat. There was lots of tension. He would yell back." There does not even seem to be a notable drive to even survive. "He would just eat a concentration rich formula and that is all he would eat a few times a day. This struggle went on until the end of the radiation in February. At the end, he lost a lot of weight."

After radiation, Mr. Shyam proceeded to surgery. In March, his doctor explained to the family that they would have to open him up to see how bad it was and he said that they might have to remove one eye. During the surgery the cancerous tissue was removed and Sunitha describes the extreme relief of them not needing to remove the one eye. But there was no going uphill. The family was yet again facing news that indicated they were up against a losing battle: "Once again, dad could not eat anything. He got an infection. . . . The doctor said they had removed most of the area but maybe not all. The cancer was not all removed. So, he went on chemotherapy again."

From May until the beginning of August, Mr. Shyam's routine would be going into hospital for three to five day stays and then being shuffled home to be cared for by his wife, daughter, and the family nanny. And the situation was still not improving. Sunitha recalls,

> By the third month we could notice there is swelling in one eye. We knew that something was wrong. He was admitted into the Apollo Hospital [a well-known and large hospital in India]. He lost his hair for the first time. Everyday they would give him some type of drug and he would run for the bathroom. At this

point he was not eating anything. After a half a year without solid food, he became almost just bones.

Mr. Shyam's journey to rock bottom is highly valuable if we can recognize in it how many of us take that same journey, in different forms, in the way we move through life challenges. He did not try anything different from what the doctors told him to do. We usually do the same, don't we? We wait for things to take their course before taking action. We are given expert advice and rely on it. We hand over our power to an authority that determines the process. Don't misunderstand. It is not giving up power to seek an expert and hear what he or she has to say or even diligently follow the advice. Giving up power is when we believe that the cure or solution lies squarely within him or her. The danger becomes manifest when we resign ourselves to that expert's assurance of hopelessness. But here is the breaking point between those who resign themselves and those who do not. Sunitha remembers,

We went to his room in the morning, my mom and me. We were sitting with him in his room. He was avoiding eye contact. He would not talk to us. We went out to the doctor, asking what is wrong, telling him nothing is working. He simply said there is a recurrence and that there is nothing they can do. And then the doctor said, 'Take him home.' We begged. They did not give us any options. My mom was crying and pushed what we can do about it. My mom never gives up. She was pleading with him despite breaking down. The doctor was not even willing to speak to us. He just repeated himself with, 'Take him home and he will die in a few days.'

## Putting Power Back Where It Belongs

Mr. Shyam and those I spoke to in the same life circumstance grabbed the keys essential to recovery. After a long and painful experience of relying on others for hope, direction, healing, and an ever more elusive victory, they embraced it for what it was gifting them with—the experience of taking back their power. They recognized the gift for a new lease on life and to fulfill their purpose. With this key in hand, they can begin to develop their whole selves. Taking back power means bringing the fractured self to wholeness.

Now Mr. Shyam was at home, too weak to even lift his head to drink and deemed soon to be dead by the doctors, so no doctor or nurse was assigned to make any house visit. It was over. But Sunitha asserts, "We are people of action. We had to do something about it." But because most people have yet to learn to take back their own power, they do not have the capacity to support others to do so. Many well-meaning friends and family came to the house to see Mr. Shyam but here was the problem Sunitha identifies.

> Hindus have all these powders. They go to the temple and bring it. Muslim friends came as well . . . everyone prayed. But their prayers were misdirected . . . the guy was still alive and all were acting as if he is going any second. You can't be rude to guests. You have to give them something to drink. My mom diligently put all these people's 'good-bye' and 'well-wishing' items and concoctions under his pillow. Then one day he just threw everything out yelling he can't sleep.

Success does not come about relying on potions or material things. Giving all hope to items is the same as giving all hope to an expert who fails you, regardless of what properties they might possess. There is no difference. Activism for this family was relying both on God and action. They started phoning all sorts of doctors. However, doctors refused to consider the case with the assessment that it would just be a matter of a couple of days for him. This did not stop the family. They were going to find someone, anyone; how, they did not know. They went to Apollo Hospital not even knowing what they were hoping to find:

There was a Hungarian doctor in the Apollo hospital. We saw him while there, while on the way somewhere else. He was smiley, taking care of patients. He was the head of the wing. My mom said, 'Let's go to him.' Western doctors don't give up like our people. He said he could see us the next morning. We went the next morning. Both of us crying, we showed him everything. He said, 'I can't promise anything but I do have a team of specialists I can show these reports and check. They are a young team of doctors.' He said, 'Just wait in this room.' And he went straight over. He was gone for 10–15 minutes. He came back, and he said 'okay, the doctors will take a chance.'

Mr. Shyam was in for surgery two days later in a critical state that Sunitha described as heartbreaking. She knew that it could be a matter of a few hours before the cancer reached his brain. The surgery lasted eighteen hours. It was a success. For the first time in one year, Mr. Shyam ate solids just two days later.

## Critical Lessons

Perhaps most of us who actually succeed in taking back power need to go through the process that awakens us to this higher consciousness of standing in our own power and the gift of intention. This is a lesson that only our soul and God can know we need. But it is my hope that others might not need to go through the worst nightmares to get to this knowledge. Certainly, Mr. Shyam believes that one can understand.

There is additional insight into Mr. Shyam's story that I gathered specifically through the narration of his daughter, Sunitha. On one level, she is also learning the life lesson through her father's experience, the example of her mother and her own struggle to keep her father alive. Through her father's experience, she is honing her ability to recognize and use several keys that lead to personal power. She is adjusting herself to embrace her own life purpose, working with intent to help heal her father, garnering greater faith, and supporting his development and strengthening wholeness.

As such, there is something much more to be noted in her narration. It is not one man's trial that produced the outcome of recognizing and embracing the means to heal and succeed. The profound truth is that to succeed it often takes the participation of more than one person. In other words, the very act of taking one's rightful power out of the hands of one that intentionally or unintentionally disempowers, is often a collective endeavor.

We are told so often that personal power means something that we as individuals must possess to succeed in our goals. This is similar to the American tale of self-made individuals who relied on nothing else but themselves. It simply does not go that way. Sunitha divulges, "There were times we were in Apollo and we had to pay 50,000 rupees that very afternoon and we did not even have 1,000. Somehow God made sure we got the money. People collected charity from their friends, people we did not know." Isolated, we are less equipped. We are dependent upon one another and so when we collectively take back our power, it seems we enable the highest possibilities of success.

Can this consciousness be extended to a wider scale? This family example shows how diverse groups can form collectives for global peace. Sunitha tells me,

Mom had a small puja room in a small extension of the kitchen. . . . My father never disturbed her while she prayed. As a couple, they were always patient with each other's beliefs. They never insulted or interfered in each other's beliefs. We grew up that way. Even if there are differences, I don't think my father ever told my mother anything. Every morning she would boil milk. For Hindus, the boiling milk is a sign of prosperity. She would light the lamp and dedicate it to God. If my mom had her period or could not, my father would light the lamp, and would leave the door open to offer it to God. She has done this all her life. During his sickness, she offered God this milk for him, and believed that God would not fail her husband.

Global security and peace has everything to do with respecting, embracing, and taking action with the other.

There is great wisdom and perfect strategy in Sunitha's parents' example. Until we can reach this level of understanding and action in our own families, we cannot possibly dream of world peace and healing. Our practice and shift in perception begins from the smallest units.

Neither Mr. Shyam nor his family would likely be able to comprehend how their souls would grow during the process. Nor would they know what mission lay ahead for them. Their experience of such immense growth is now readily shared and helping many individuals who have been let down or need the help. Success is a collective responsibility. Sunitha describes,

> My parents try to spread the awareness that even at stage four cancer can be cured. They are still friends with the doctor that saved him. For them it is like a birth, but like a second life. Eighteen hours was one of the longest operations the doctors had done. Father and mother and the doctor just talked at an event telling my father's story. Now that hospital sends patients to them for counselling and my parents go in to visit some of the patients.

Although Mr. Shyam's ordeal is an individual experience, it was clearly his soul plan for not just his but wider successes. And with his new lease on life, he and his wife are busy gifting others with the key of wholeness through taking back personal power.

～

# ⤠ 15 ⤟

# Miracles: A Father's Lessons

*"I put those hard feelings all behind me, so I felt that night that she would be healed. . . . She got healed that night. I was right in front of her."*

## Introduction

Prayer, and the opening of our hearts that it demands for forgiveness and compassion, is one of the most important keys for assuring real success. Our material world is determined by our connection to Source and, therefore, what we can bring into this world. Our physical world takes shape by the Light and compassion we bring into it. If it is our life that needs healing, we need only ask. If it is someone else's, we can ask, too. We will receive what illuminates our hearts and, therefore, the world. In fact, as we will learn in the following story the illumination of one area creates ripple effects even with nonlocality. All we need to do is ask and open ourselves in earnest. God's power will enter our lives; we become witnesses to changes in our lives and actually, the lives of others.

In fact, miracles are possible. When we pray, the heavens quickly align to help us. Through prayer, we do receive our deepest desires in accordance with God's plan for our good and our joy. Heaven wants to give us what we truly desire in alignment with our highest good. That is in accordance with our ultimate purpose. But too many of us ask and do not believe. We ask and we continue to hate or fear. We ask and then we go and give over power to something else. One must remove all such barriers that block experiencing God's grace. If we do not remove these barriers, how can we hope for real success? God always hears and responds but when we close ourselves to receiving, we then say that God never heard our prayer. A young woman, Amber Rix, and her family, provides us great lessons of the miracles of prayer.

### Amber's Lazy Eye

I remember being introduced to the new member of the family, Amber. And later, I can also recall Amber's eyes being "different" and the explanation that she had "lazy eye." At the time, no one could know what this condition would entail, the long and painful ordeal the family would soon undergo and then the immense blessings and lessons that can come out of such a situation. We often do not realize it when staring into the eyes of a baby what immense burden and what grand missions may be in store.

One of the great lessons for her may have been to grow strong. Yet, today her trial has become a lesson for others. I believe her sacrifice was to teach another soul, her father, much more than growing strong. Now, he can truly attest to the power of prayer and the process of faith, an integral lesson that often requires alchemizing of the self to truly understand. The "lazy eye" transformed later into an even greater test that pushed the entire family to experience what it really means to forgive, access God's power and grace through prayer. In their experience is great wisdom for many more of us to be gained. In turning to God in prayer and bringing love and compassion into our world, we can all develop a higher understanding of how to succeed in life.

Koreen, Amber's mother, shares, "When Amber was about three, I noticed that especially one eye drifted." Her father, George, explains that they noticed Amber was looking in another direction on an angle and tilting her head. Growing worried, they decided to take her to an optometrist to find out what was going on. When she went, the optometrist asked her questions. She was tested to see how she saw things in numbers and colors. It was discovered that she saw things blurry. Hearing the test results, Koreen turned to Amber and asked her if it was always like that. She replied, "Yah, I thought everyone saw like that."

Koreen shares that they called it "lazy eye." One eye was a dominant eye, so they patched the dominant eye in an attempt to make the other eye work. Later the doctors said she had something called, esotropia, where both eyes were affected. One eye was to the side and the other tilted up from birth. The doctors used surgery to turn the eyes to focus straight ahead.

## Surgery Gone Wrong

George proceeded to tell what transpired,

> She had the surgery. The next day we noticed the eyes were even further out! They had operated on the wrong eye! [The doctors switched instructions for each eye, meaning that they did the required operation for the left eye on the right and vice

versa]. When they found out that they operated on the wrong eyes [one at a time], they did a second surgery one week later to correct the first operations' surgery. Then the eye was patched after the second operation. Amber had to adjust her head to focus her eyes downward because of the wrong adjustments. They had to re-operate on the eyes and we waited another six months for them to operate. They operated again when she was six years old and then when she was nine years old. Then they would not, to avoid making matters worse. When she was about 10, the doctor said to her, 'Do you see double?' She said, 'Yes.'

Through all these operations on *both* eyes, the young Amber patiently endured and never complained. Koreen inquired why she didn't say that she had double vision, and Amber simply replied, "Well, don't you?" She never realized that it was not normal to see in doubles. George tells how he tried to grapple with what was happening,

I was upset. I was mad at the end. Because you would think in my experience if you do something that serious. . . . I do carpentry and I check myself. I double-check the different angles etcetera. But this guy didn't until after the operation. He read the prescription but did the wrong eyes. He moved the eyes back as far as he could to 'get it right.' The eyes were so far out!

I kept this anger in my head all these years. Amber went back again maybe three years later and he checked her eyes again. She was having this downward gaze to get her eyes to focus right. And she has been doing that now since she was seven, and now she is 25. I said to Koreen, 'We should have her checked again; maybe with modern technology we can get this right. They said they couldn't do more than that.

*The Miracle*

George's struggle to understand is the central perspective offered here in the years of Amber's struggle. It is a significant one because it is an aspect of a whole journey of these souls together as a family. On a soul level, Amber pushed George's to undergo what it needed in order to grow. His growth in turn is what contributed to the transformation of the whole family's experience materially and spiritually. We can know in his example just how inextricably connected we truly are as families, communities, and the world and, therefore, how powerful we are to transform the whole. The barriers that George had to break down to allow God to do His work are the same barriers we all need to break down to finally experience the flow of Spirit's power through us. We can know how George dissolved the barrier to receiving and the resulting miracles of healing. He tells me,

> We have been praying for her for years to get some help from the Lord. We had prayed for many people. So, I guess that I thought many times about how I felt about this guy. One day Pastor Yadon preached on. He said that we really need to forgive our enemies and those people that hurt us because the Bible says that if we do not forgive we are not

forgiven, and that is really important to your lives as Christians. If we keep ourselves as unforgiving in our hearts it is a hindrance in our worship with God. When he preached that the second time, I decided to forgive him [the doctor]. He is not alive anymore so I realized that I am only hurting myself.

At camp meeting this year I really prayed and cried out to the Lord to heal her because I had made sure I had forgiven this guy. I put those hard feelings all behind me, so I felt that night that she would be healed. She was not healed that night. She was also praying. She was also praying for Jessica, my daughter-in-law. That was Wednesday. On Thursday, this young preacher's wife, who knows Amber and has been praying for her and Jessica both, came up to her. She told Amber that she would be healed. She said that she had received a message [through Divine communication] that she will be healed, and that Jessica will also be healed.

I didn't know that 'til the next day, Friday service. I was praying again for her and so many people were praying for her, too. I thought maybe she got healed on Wednesday because I felt that and maybe she didn't tell anyone. Other people told her the same, that she would be healed. Judy Leaman said to Amber, "Friday night, Amber your healing is here right now." Several people came around to pray.

She got healed that night. I was right in front of her. People came up and questioned her. She was looking around her and didn't know what to say. She said, "I think I'm healed!" Shortly after that, many other people came up and prayed with her as well.

It wasn't very long before the whole campground came and knew she was healed and thanked the Lord for this healing.

## How Miracles Work

George asked me, "Can you imagine if that was Sarah [my daughter] and you could not do anything about it?" I am self-aware that it often takes my seeing how a situation touches me directly or placing my own child or myself in the situation to feel more deeply and grasp more fully the gravity and difficulty of the test. In his example, however, I have also been reminded of the barriers, which we erect in our own hearts, not just in our material world and yet foolishly continue to think we can change the world when we build the barriers ourselves.

For several years, George was holding onto resentment towards the doctor who had made such a significant mistake with his little girl. Through forgiveness, he enabled the miracle. Put in the same challenge, would I really know how to reach the depth of compassion and understanding necessary to transmute the pain and sever the ropes of unforgiveness that enmeshed and bound everyone? I asked him straight out to explain how he did his part. He describes his path,

> It did make me bitter. I just prayed to ask the Lord to forget about this and forgive. You really have to mean it. I used to be really upset and sour. I am actually healed, healed from the weight that was on my mind about this. So, of course it makes my life better and people who are around me 'cause it just upset me. So, I would encourage people to have a little

more faith in God and maybe pray more. We need to pray and be serious about it because it is serious.

It is now six weeks since Amber was fully healed. She is a happy and healthy young woman and her parents attest to her happiness. For all these years, Amber was in severe pain because of the way she held her shoulders and twisted her neck in order to do her homework and read, which created chronic strain in her neck and shoulder muscles. Her parents tirelessly put a heat pad on her sore muscles every night until she did this herself, every single night for years. Even through the pain and the suffering, it was never Amber who complained. Amber tended to her studies, her work and life in a way that anyone who knows her would be truly humbled and inspired by. It was her father (and mother) who held the pain and resentment. He confirms, "She doesn't need to do this [add heat at night]. She can see straight now. Doctors can't do it. But God can do it. I can't be any happier for her, my little girl."

Certainly, God wants us to have what we ache for. It is then part of His plan for us to learn how to achieve what we want and how to open ourselves to Him to receive. And when we do our part by moving closer and opening to let His Light in, heaven helps. Amber's healing is surely a miracle. Yet, as her father has shown, it required a number of critical yet simple steps to allow God to do His work of miracles.

## Steps Towards Miracles

First, George came to full acknowledgement of his *responsibility* in holding a human being who had already passed over in his thoughts as unforgivable and, thereby, harmed not the doctor but himself for many years. Part of having relinquished responsibility is due to George transferring some of the responsibility he placed on the doctor who made the mistake to other doctors. He could only imagine that doctors could mend what had happened. In blaming and then misplacing hope, he had effectively given over power, which resulted in him feeling utterly dependent and increasingly hopeless. He became conscious of his misplacement of power and hope upon listening to a preacher. In self-realization of what he was doing, he could see where that got him but then also where he wanted to go. He made the decision that he did not want to feel the pain he was feeling anymore and did not want his family to be burdened even more. From this basis for choosing, he chose to want to feel God's blessings, be free and for all to experience health. He was ready to manifest the new.

Second, George made an *intention* for creating the new. He decided on what he wanted. The doctor had passed over. George and his family still had their lives to live. He needed a different approach, a different story. This change was now clear in his mind and conviction. Much like a director of a movie, George decided it was time for a different scene, a scene that would be healthier. The point had come for George to decide to change scenes and changing scenes means to take back power.

Third is *action*. He acted upon his intention. For this man, action required redirecting the focus of massive amounts of energy. What we are focusing on internally is what we feed energy into, thereby, creating more of. The source of pain and the hope was the doctors who eventually told him they could no longer offer him hope. Yet, he was continuing the process of pain felt and experienced by focusing on this source for years and years. No more would he stare at the pain. He kept his heart and mind focused on what God can and wants to deliver. Through time, he then was able to change the frequency at which his heart, mind, and actions were operating. He tells me that God was empowering him on every level.

In redirecting energy, George tapped into the power of forgiveness and then prayer. He emptied himself of the dark energies that were holding himself and everyone back from moving forward. He made the intention and will to finally forgive. He says, "You really have to mean it . . . be serious about it." With firm intention, he turned to his Lord for help. He did not merely ask first for Amber's healing. He took the crucial step before Amber's healing and asked for the help to forgive.

Asking God to help forgive is telling heaven that we want to do it together and that we are now ready to do our part. This surrendering enables a process of trust and faith, essential ingredients for letting go and receiving assistance. When we clear and purify ourselves, we open up for God to sweep through us and into our lives. We must be ready and willing to finally let it go and "forget" and submit to real power. Obviously, George remembers. But, the act to choose to "forget" entails letting go of the focus on despair and unforgiveness and shifting the heart and mind, bit by bit, to optimism and compassion.

The key to understanding how powerful we are in creating change beyond ourselves is in self-awareness and understanding our feelings, our being, and the connection we have to All That Is. Because we form a collective consciousness and our energies vibrate with those around us, everyone in the family or collective is entangled in a way or degree. In accordance with that principle of connectedness, George had to heal before his daughter could be healed. George had to release resistance within himself in order to accept Light and compassion. He tells, "I was healed from the weight that was on my mind about this." He intuitively knew he could not simply turn to God and expect a miracle when his heart is closed off. When he freed himself, so was his family. When he forgave, he says, "I felt that night that she would be healed." Not only George, but on the following day others received messages that the time had come for Amber to be healed, and then on the second day, she was. George confirms,

> It is a relief for the whole family, not just Amber. It also lifted Koreen from this burden as well. What if there are people in your life you have not asked for forgiveness? So, you ask your Lord to forgive others for you that you have held in your mind, and that will give your mind more liberty again. Without that liberty you are still not free.

> This happiness has spread to all the family, extended family and all her friends from school. They all knew her as looking a certain way. They are all touched. Even though she has always been an upbeat and happy person, she is even a happier person.

When we pray fully, the rest is left up to God. Prayer helps skip many wavelengths to accessing the higher realms and creating miracles when we submit our inner resistance and simply allow. In this was a lesson—prayer works miracles with forgiveness and "a little more faith in God."

George and his wife now have an evolved perspective. Miracles were at some time foreign occurrences to them, but now they are firm believers in the power of prayer. For many of us, miracles still seem abnormal. That is understandable given that we are taught in so many subtle and direct ways to disregard our own power and Source. I believe that more miracles will be noticed and manifested as more of us work on breaking down our barriers that block our ability to believe—as George has shown us. However, as his experience demonstrates, believing comes about not in a sudden attempt, but often by working with time, even failure, in moving towards acceptance and expectation. Koreen has now seen numerous miraculous and instant healings take place and so she simply believes. But she once did not believe at all. She tells of her first encounter with the power of prayer,

> The first time I experienced a miraculous healing was when I was working [as a nurse] one evening [approximately three decades ago] and a lady in her seventies was dying of cancer. She was a First Nations lady who was old but didn't look her age, who had been unconscious for six days. Several people visited her. They made such noise for hours and hours. I went down to tell them that that was it, it is late and it's time to go home. I went back to my work.
>
> In her room the alarm went off. So, I headed to her room and entered to find her sitting up in her bed. She asked for a cup of tea. I was shocked. Then I made a correlation between all that ruckus and prayer and her miraculous healing. She left the

hospital just a few days later. She was well, eating and drinking right away. We just kept her for a few days to be sure. She died two years later but not of cancer.

Belief in God's power rather than giving over our power to those who help erect blockages in belief and in being demands a journey towards Source. It is important, therefore, that you be patient with yourself as you push yourself along this journey to eventually believe with your whole self.

*Ripple Effects*

The power that one gains from this journey affects not only your life but the many others who will need miracles in their lives, too. This is because all of life is interconnected. Where one part undergoes change in any system, here being one family, another part will be touched—the extended family. George spoke of Jessica, his daughter-in-law, who lives in California with their son, Ryan. She started healing at about the same time.

As we awaken in our hearts and minds, we awaken much more around us. New ground covered in quantum physics tells us of the power of influencing healing in others in completely different localities by merely our own changes in our own systems or bodies. Much is yet to be researched in how much power we have in changing localities beyond our own places of living by changing ourselves. One of the persons who informed Amber's family that she would be healed channeled a message at the same time that Jessica would be healed. George tells me,

She started healing in a different way. Seven months later now the doctors still don't know what is wrong with her. When we were down in California in February, she just could not function anymore, getting dizzy spells, headaches, she couldn't walk far, she would get weak, and then she couldn't do anything. She had to cancel the rest of her semester at school and for over six months she has been to many doctors and many hospitals in different places. She had to be carried sometimes. She couldn't walk.

When they put her in the hospital, she had really high pressure at the low end, way over a hundred. In fact they kept her in the hospital in Sacramento and so the alarm would go off each time it hit 105. They have done many, many things on her. They have had cardiologists, urologists, psychologists. She had a little swelling at the back of the brain. They gave her something for it and it shrank, but she was still sick. They focused on her heart, etcetera. She went home. A doctor in San Francisco decided that they better check her over again doing the exact same things. They found the same things as before with no explanation as to why her low-end pressure was going all wonky.

She has been waiting the last couple of months for some word, and then she started getting better two weeks after she was to get healed. About a week ago, she texted and said, "I drove to Starbucks today!" The doctors still have not figured it out [her miraculous healing]. They had tried all kinds of things. She had not driven for seven months!

George illustrates the exponential power of healing. In such an example we can know the power that one can resort to by moving inward and clearing, going forward and asking—and for things we have erroneously thought we cannot have, and finally allowing God to do His miraculous work, all within Divine order and God's pleasure for us. Having raised his own vibrations in this process, he, his family, and their community are awakening others to the same truth.

This awakening enables true empowerment and change. Jessica drove to Starbucks and let them know in gratitude how empowered and thrilled she is. They are showing us it is a process that takes work and belief, but in steps we all have and can access that same power. We can all have the same empowerment, joy, and fulfillment. Our own empowerment, joy, and fulfillment are the way—our calling to contribute the same to the world around us. George affirms,

> It appears to me that she [Jessica] is getting better. I believe that it is our faith and our prayers and maybe it is partly our own attitude towards it all [sickness and healing]. [Several months later she is now doing full-time study and working.] Even this thing about forgiveness, maybe it is more people who have more faith. Wanda, it all comes down to faith, really, because faith will make you well, faith will make you whole.

∼

# ⮞ 16 ⮜

# Through Addiction: Learning about Greed, Power, and Peace

*"I find that love and therefore forgiveness, compassion, and faith are the truth to all healing throughout all nations and people and religions. Indians [Northern Tutchone] call it dooli."*

## Introduction

Success is overcoming a challenge in life. Greater success comes from gaining wisdom from that experience. Even greater is the wisdom to use that challenge to be able to help others and live life in service of the Divine. Andy Nieman illustrates all these successes. He was homeless, often sleeping on street concrete and eating out of garbage cans. He was an alcoholic for twenty-seven years and a cocaine addict for twenty-three years. He further spent several years sticking heroine up his arm. He reached a point at which his body was to give out on him. The major keys he uses to get through such a long, enduring experience, survive, and succeed is faith in the Divine, love, forgiveness, and a wider concept of justice.

## Ripped Away from Home

It is no surprise that Andy became alcoholic and turned to drugs. A good number of Native people have come forward with their personal stories and told how their anguished childhood on a residential school pushed them to drown their suffering and pain through drinking. Andy is also First Nations and experienced living on a residential school when he was a child. In 2013, the Truth and Reconciliation Commission in Canada organized to hear the stories of 150,000 individuals, which is a long awaited critical step in the process of healing. Although some organizations have formed to provide support and healing, too many spirits have continued broken, without the keys to surpass such traumatic childhood experience. Only in 2008 had the government provided an official apology to the First Nations, Inuit, and Metis.

An important chapter of Canadian history is the residential schools that were created to "civilize the Indians." Native children were physically ripped away from their homes and their parents and were then placed in these boarding schools created by the government and administered by Christian churches. Although they began in the early 19th century, the last government run residential school closed as recently as 1996. The purpose was to assimilate the natives into a Eurocentric view of civilization, essentially after their colonization. Survivors recall the systematic means of assimilation through the teachers repeating to the children that their culture, religion, language, and sometimes even the way they looked was bad. Numerous stories have brought to light the regular sexual molestation and physical abuse. In childhood, numerous little spirits were broken this way. Andy tells me, "I was ten when I went there and fourteen when I left. From then on, I was on skid row for over ten years and ten and a half years in different jails."

Andy had the childhood trauma of being ripped from family, endured physical abuses and molestation of the residence, the systematic government program of erasing identity and sense of selfhood, and then substance addiction and the related habits to overcome. Andy had all the cards stacked against him.

## Faith for Overcoming Addiction

I ask Andy Nieman how he overcame his ordeal.

I used trust in God to overcome all this. Humility—being humble enough to talk about what happened to me. Courage and honesty—most of my life I lived on lies as my only way of having control. If people didn't know about me I had control over them. So, saying the way I felt, not having to hide and not pretending that everything is okay when it is not, not saying something is the way it isn't. Compassion—God's compassion and forgiveness. Forgiveness is a big one—God forgiving me and me forgiving others. You forgive others as a way to forgive yourself. The Bible says to give honor unto all men. That means all men, all people. So, I don't pick and choose who I'm going to honor and who I am not going to honor. I am going to honor all people including the one that abused me, the one that hurt me. So that helped me to forgive myself and others. Obeying the Bible where it says 'honor all men' helped me. It allowed me to work with sexual offenders, men involved in violence, and pedophiles. There are really no bad people; there are just people that make bad choices.

I did so many bad things; I hurt so many people. If God can forgive me for all the bad stuff that I did, surely I can forgive others. Who am I to say God forgave me for all things, but I can't forgive you that one thing? There is no balance in that. If God can forgive me, then I can forgive you. Because He made us in his image, he was put on the cross and he was able to forgive, we have the understanding and example that it goes back to honoring all men. God is no respecter of personalities. He is not going to forgive one and not the other. He loves us all.

Faith in the Divine is an incredibly powerful key to move through such challenges. Andy could move through his pain, guilt, and deep sense of loss by trusting that God would help him achieve his goal. He gave over his burdens and relied on something larger than himself. But there is yet a larger key. If we miss it to start, all other keys are simply much more difficult to grasp. Andy shares, "I did it for Him. . . . I tried AA (Alcoholics Anonymous), Narcotics Anonymous. I did it for my mom, to keep my girlfriends, my job. But when I did it for God, that is what made the difference."

Andy Nieman is a husband and father. He earned a university degree in social work, founded and heads an organization to counsel youth to heal from difficult childhoods, is a member of his local government, a poet, and an ordained minister. He is, furthermore, a published author, having written on his experience and healing.

Alcoholism and drug abuse continues to have a strangle-hold on many native households as a result of a collective loss of heritage, autonomy, and way of life. He now dedicates his waking hours to service in helping those move forward in life and teaching spiritual principles.

*Healing the Next Generation*

Andy has been able to help and heal now thousands of youth. He knows how to do it. I have also spoken at length to other counselors in the communities who are frustrated with their efforts and continue to grapple with the growing number of youth who are struggling to find their way from within the context of generational substance abuse and the various and numerous related social, emotional, mental, and physical issues. They try very hard and most are well educated in counseling methods, as well as the context of the situation. Perhaps the intricate problem is much larger than most of these professionals can reasonably handle. However, more significantly, as in most professions, we are apt to holding onto rational objective approaches that simply cannot get to the heart of the issues we are addressing. As problems, such as these, increase, the fallacy of our approaches will become even more evident.

I ask him how he has such tremendous success in guiding the youth to empowerment, healing, and right paths. He explains, "I have been through it. This automatically creates trust in others who are going through it. I have a trust I don't even have to earn. People already know what I have been through. They want to go to the heart of the problem. Trust is there, a high level of trust, so they are able to take steps."

### Restorative Justice Critical to Healing

Andy suggests steps for healing that are truly sustainable. He has gained the wisdom of the right steps through overcoming his ordeal, wisdom he gained from his experience in punishment and mercy, wisdom from his ancestral teachings and Christian teachings as well. He explains that the basis for all healing from trauma and life challenges is love. From love, forgiveness, compassion, and faith grow and nurture the soul. He explains, however, that these are universal principles that work for everybody. The goal of working with this set of universal principles is to restore wholeness, healing, and, at the same time, balance through justice. Andy explains,

> I find that love and therefore forgiveness, compassion and faith is the truth to all healing throughout all nations and people and religions. Indians [Northern Tutchone] call it *dooli*. General society calls it what goes around comes around. The Bible says what you sow is what you reap. That is a universal law that has been established by God and that is one thing that is in the First Nations' belief system. *Dooli*, which means if you are bad to someone that bad will come back to you, if you kill an animal you give thanks for it or else you will not be successful next time. There is respect for the land and animals. What I like about First Nations' culture and philosophy is that before contact with others, there was the saying that 'it takes a whole community to raise a child.' If we go back forty years ago, if we see a child running around late anyone could call and say 'come get your child.' But this way of dealing has been lost. First Nations used to have their

government system whereby the whole family was accountable. If I killed someone in your family, you could choose someone from our family to die, or be banished or could pay us something. But it was a community thing, in which the family paid. Yet, the community decided.

They started a thing called circle sentencing or restorative justice. Today's system is punitive. But we try to restore the victim and perpetrator. So we include all family and community and the sentence is that so-and-so has to cut wood for the elders or has to do so many hours of community work, or has to go to a certain program, counseling. Within this community agreement, one will say, 'I'll drive him or her.' It is also about restitution to the family. In the circle, the offender has to face the victim if the victim is willing and has an opportunity to speak to the offender. It is so hard to hear from the person you have hurt. The government system now does not have that. The person goes in and does days and comes out, but no healing takes place. Restorative justice has taken the backburner because it takes more resources to heal a person and the government is not willing to do that. It was going really good for a few years in the Yukon but there were not enough resources although the community is trying to keep it going.

Restorative justice is a significantly important approach that uses a higher notion of intelligence and pragmatism in creating the means for wholeness and healing, critically beginning with the individual. As Andy stresses, it is an essential practice in order for humanity to progress. The concept of a higher notion of justice is recognized as absolutely indispensible in the last chapter in which compassionate justice is discussed as a similar alternative to that provided by existing systems, alternatives which will be crucial for humanity to advance and world peace to become more tangible.

## Love of Money, Pride, Land, and its Resources

Resources or, more accurately, the love of resources, poses the problem here. At the individual level, the love of money and the issue of pride serve as a major barrier for the ability to support higher concepts of justice. Andy stresses, "The big thing you would have to do away with is the love of money and pride. Pride and power are tied in." He explains, "When you look at wars, it is usually over land and resources which are tied into money." Andy is right. He and two further contributors to knowledge on spiritual activism included within, Robert Crane and Dane Wigington, all stress that the biggest block to humanity's progress is greed over land and resources. These thinkers and spiritual activists have identified the most significant barrier and source of various wars going on today. They all provide more sustainable solutions. Here Andy provides his.

He explains importantly that individuals, communities, and governments must find sustainable solutions for overcoming greed. For him, this is the only way forward for humanity to successfully overcome current wars and the growing inequalities fuelling wars. He also recognizes that right conduct is part of universal law that applies to the individual and all levels, and stresses that these commandments must be supported by governments.

I have always wondered how some beautiful activists who have worked so hard in their more youthful and innocent years later turn corrupt. Yes, these include people I have squarely placed as spiritual activists. I have come across several who now support entities that provide them with large sums of money, forms of luxury, and/or greater power and influence. Andy answers this for me. He explains, "There are three things that will change even the most respectful person. One is money, the other is sex, and the third is authority. Those three are the top. You could come up to a person and say particular people would never do awful things that harm others, but these three things can change them." These three come from the same energy of greed for resources. The various expressions of greed over resources that we easily identify and are more apt to accuse others of submitting to in larger groups and corporations becomes manifest, however, first through individuals choosing to work with the energy of coercive power, which is power over people and things.

I ask Andy to suggest further how a higher form of justice can be secured so that we can still heal humanity and enable world peace. He tells me, "If everyone in the world followed the Ten Commandments we would have world peace. God put the Ten Commandments in Exodus, chapter 20. If you read those and if everyone did, we would have world peace. There would be enough food, people would get along and there would be no wars." This endeavor begins with an individual commitment to justice and right action. The Ten Commandments are the most basic rules for right conduct that all religions uphold in essence. However, Andy emphasizes that, "it would take world governments cooperating."

The odds of peace are clearly present. Peace is possible and there are steps to achieve it. It can be made possible through first purging or purifying individual greed. Alignment with God's will for ensuring right conduct follows. We still need authority to support this process within a clear framework of a higher form of justice. This must be one that relies firstly on community authority and one that uses the means of restoring and healing. Government must be present, despite the fact that government has not served this role thus far. However, it must be in the capacity as supporter and facilitator of this community and individual commitment to justice. Otherwise, government, as any individual, functions within the energy of greed. When we are at this level of self-discipline, conduct and cooperation with community and government, larger corporations and monopolies that many governments and individuals now attend to cannot have the leverage they do now in creating greater inequality and strife. The systems that uphold greed would crumble.

∼

# ☙ 17 ❧

# From Poverty and Abandonment to Service in Humanity

*"If I give to other people, God gives me what I need. If you give to other people, I believe God gives you double. I tell others to give who tell me not to give."*

## Introduction

I learned that Rowena had lost her aunt this morning. She continues her day in tears. This news is just one among a lifetime of events. The following is an account of a young woman who has endured an unfathomable number of unrelenting trials in her life. Life has squeezed her. The major key she uses to grow is foremost remembrance in the Divine and therefore faith in the Divine. Importantly, through all of life's trials she had resolved and chosen to strive and work ardently with the law of love key. Few people I have crossed paths with exemplify selfless service as she does.

Her aunt was sick for some time so it is not an entire shock, but her aunt played a loving role in her life and her loss is painful. Rowena just lost her uncle less than a week ago. Her uncle, only forty-three, and his wife, thirty-nine, were killed in an accident leaving ten children behind with the youngest two-and-half-years old, which Rowena offered to adopt. Two days before this, her fourteen-year-old nephew who she was trying to help through a painful experience ran away. Some months ago she lost her sister she was closest to in age and friendship and just a month before that another uncle, a political dissident, was murdered in plain sight after dropping off his daughter at the same school Rowena's daughter goes to. Her pain today, as this entire year, is cumulative and, so, unbearable. Welcome to Rowena Dagaang's life path. Hers is illustrative of the meaning derived from a life of struggle and real success in choosing to give selflessly.

I know that tomorrow she will wake up and continue to give of herself. No matter what happens, Rowena has continued to give, giving guidance and ideas, giving whatever material things she can. She is often told that she does not think like other people. I identified immediately why—she operates more often from the perspective of her soul. She will be giving almost everything she gains materially to whoever she thinks needs it more and turning in deep devotion and prayer between and upon any such news. She literally lives on next to nothing, just enough, and consistently gives every penny she has away, first as a single mother to support her six-year-old daughter to have the education she never got, and also for the education and meals for other children. She is not a billionaire or one who does it for acclaim, so her every day form of giving will garner attention—far from it. She works very hard as a nanny in the Arab Gulf away from her daughter and family in the Philippines. Her actions are simple and, in fact, discreet, but filled with so much of her. Indeed, if every human being contributed acts of selfless love in the same way, the world would be an entirely different place.

## Childhood Abandonment

Her life path and learning are, however, instructive. Rowena tells her story.

> My father died when I was two and a half and mother when I was seventeen. When my father died, all of us [six children] went different directions. One sister was already married. From the time I was three I was living in different houses, at my aunt's, cousin's, sometimes on the street when they got mad at me. When my mother remarried six months after my father died [to a man who had some eight or nine wives], my sister didn't let me go with my mom to my stepfather's house. But when my mother left to be with her husband, nobody cared for me. By six years old, I was already on the street. When my brother beat me, for example, I would just run away and sleep under a coconut tree or mango tree. They would find me sometimes three days later. I would just eat the coconut.

> I met an old lady who found me on the street when I was seven years old. She told me to come with her to sell vegetables. She said that she would have one basket and I would have one. The money I would make from my basket would be mine to keep. So, in the early morning every day before school, I would go and sell vegetables on the street with her. From that work I paid for my elementary school fees until year six. One of my brothers

would push me; in fact, he would beat me if he found out I skipped school.

I did not always make enough money for school. Once, when I was nine, I gathered all the eggs the hens had laid from my rich aunt. I stole them and sold them. I did that to pay for the school uniform. My teacher said that if I did not have a uniform, I could not enter the school. Up until then I had borrowed a uniform from my classmate. When my aunt discovered I stole the eggs, she put me in a type of jail in the middle of the town for ten days. I had asked her and her husband, my uncle, for just twenty-five cents earlier and they wouldn't even give me that.

When I entered high school [from grade seven], I worked for a teacher in their house for cleaning. But his wife cut my hair completely off, so I ran away. I kept looking for work, such as at a factory for bread, putting bread in plastic bags, different jobs like that. I was seven and eight years old. I did that until I finished year seven. Then I was twelve years old.

When my stepfather died, my mother came back, so I lived with my mom, but she had asthma and was very sick by that time. So I stopped school just to work to take care of her. But I would still go to the school and stand by the window and listen. I couldn't pay and so I could not enroll. I would go every single day. One day, the teacher thought I was a student and called me to get in the classroom and join the class. I was able to attend in the classroom for almost the whole year. But when she found out that I had not enrolled, she kicked me out. The principal found out and came to my house to offer to take me to her home so that I could work for her. She would then allow me into the school. But I told her that I can't, I have to take care of my mom. So I continued working to support my mom. I tried to continue standing by the window of the classroom of my schoolmates, but then security was tightened and alerted to look out for me. At thirteen years old, I continued doing work as a housemaid.

At a house, there was another housemaid. The other girl's father was sick. She was eleven years old. So, I told her I would send her to school as long as she would stay with my mother to help out while I work longer hours to do that. She stayed with my mother and me until my mother died. I continued to contribute to her school all the way to when she graduated from high school. I felt like an older sister to her. She finished her school. I found the girl on Facebook recently. She even went on to university. When some of my siblings found out that I had paid for her school all those years, they were so angry.

*Two Pivotal Moments: Assumed Dead and Accused of Immorality*

Rowena's drive to keep moving forward and give to others comes from a consciousness of God. She knows for sure she is never alone and that God and His universe are on her side. When I asked her if I could use her story, she was reluctant at first. She thought that she still has far to go on her path to getting over her parents dying so early in her life and especially her mother's abandonment. She has shared that she is still trying to learn why God let that happen, and why her parents did that. No, we are not perfect and we do not understand it all. That is the whole point. We need to grow as souls and submit in faith, and because that is our imperative and God's will, we are perfect.

Rowena illustrates precisely how success is an ongoing process. We are in the process to grow; therefore, we have to use those life experiences and moments in our lives that train us to remember to choose healing, service, expressing our unique selves, giving, and trusting. We all have those experiences and moments of our own for our own unique path of growth and service.

There are two events that helped Rowena on her path to service. Foremost, through these she knows without any doubt that she is not alone and that there is a God. These experiences remind her to be conscious to always choose service and right actions. The first experience goes back to the time of her father's death when she was two and a half. She was in the hospital with her father, mother, and several relatives as he was dying. She was lying in the same bed because, as it so happened, she had chicken pox so bad, as she was told, that she, too, was dying. Somehow both she and her father were pronounced dead at the same time. It seems their souls synchronistically left their bodies at the same moment. In fact, enough time had passed for the news to go out to all relatives that both had died.

She describes this event,

I remember I was floating, floating upwards where I could see everything below. Then I moved outside the room and hospital to the street. I could see everything outside the hospital. And then I moved on. My father was then with me but ahead of me. He was calling to me to come. He said to come several times. But a voice down below was calling me back. It was telling me to come. So, I told my father that I will come back to him but I just need to go to that voice first. He said, 'If you choose that then I want to tell you that I planted a lily plant for you outside your window [window of her home]. Every time you want me to be close to you, the lilies will remind you that I am with you. The flower is with you, so you don't feel alone ever.'

Rowena sadly remembers that he knew that she couldn't go with him. But she also affirms that she feels that she has a special connection with her father that lives on. She confirms that she knows that through everything she is not alone. This occurrence she attests, importantly, proved to her that there is an Afterlife. She tells that throughout her childhood she always dreamed of angels, which also proved to her that she was not alone and protected by God.

Another event would play a role in her expanded awareness.

I was living with my niece [around the same age as Rowena, in adulthood] while her husband was away working in Saudi Arabia. Her mother is my stepsister. Her daughter was just a baby then. I would look after her daughter when she was out. But then she was out nearly every night. There were times she was away for three days and she would just tell me to keep an eye on her daughter. I knew she had a boyfriend. Actually, she was with many different men. But she tried to hide them from me. She was afraid that I would tell her husband when he returned. In fact, once when he did come home she sent me away for the whole time he was home.

One day, she sent a text message by mistake to her husband, which she wrote for her boyfriend. Her husband called immediately and asked what was going on. She told him that it was aunty [Rowena] who was using her phone to send that message to her boyfriend and she sent it to him by mistake. I never found out what was in that message but whatever it was it made him so disgusted with me. In fact, it went to other family members that I had a boyfriend and was acting in an unacceptable way. It was inappropriate as well because I was also a new mother [albeit single mother].

I tried telling the family that it wasn't me, that it was her. I tried to get her to stop her behavior and asked the family to step in to get her to stop. That made things worse. The whole family, including her, accused me of trying to ruin her marriage by spreading lies. In fact, my sister beat me in front of lots of people because of it. Nobody believed me. And the family was concerned that I would wrongly cause a divorce from a man that had lots of money.

I asked God to show them that I am innocent, that it was my niece. God is always there for me. He knew I was innocent. They thought I, aunty, was fooling around with men. She had a lot of men. I continued to try to advise her. I continued to take care of her daughter. But I prayed that God would reveal that I am innocent. I told everyone, 'Even if you all don't believe me I know that I am not alone, God is with me and God believes me.' What kept me going is the idea I held onto that God reveals all things, and from the time my father died I believed that I would not be let down, but just to be patient and wait. I believe in karma, too. I know that if I ever did something wrong I know that I will get the karma right away. My sister now tells me I'm not human because I live my life this way. Then, I held onto faith that God would not let me down.

Then it happened. She got pregnant, of course while her husband was away. She went and got an abortion. The doctor who did the abortion was her husband's cousin. She didn't know. Her husband came home. I was around this time. He just kept silent the whole time. During his stay, he gathered more information. Then he went straight, got a divorce and flew back to Saudi.

It was revealed to the family. This proved to me that karma is very real, that it will come and that the truth must always show, even if it takes a long time. All I could do the whole time was keep praying that God gets me through it all. This showed me that God never lets me down. I am never alone.

### Defining and Living Real Success

Rowena's dream is to be a teacher. Yet, she did not go further than grade seven. Still, every year when she is home in the Philippines, teachers call her in to teach. She is offering skills and approaches these few teachers appreciate. There are always problems when other teachers find out because they fear that due to regulations they can get into trouble. But she loves it, the teachers push her to teach, and she never passes up an opportunity to contribute. She tells me that a few years ago she gathered a group of activists and explained to them that they should open a part-time school to teach religion to children, and she outlined how to do it.

A year later when she returned she was surprised and overjoyed to find that her motivation and little contribution of ideas had gone a long way. Her ideas were taken and put into action. A part-time makeshift school was erected and was already full to capacity. She explains that her aspirations are really to go beyond trying to help materially. She says, "I am trying to teach them and that's the place and age I want to be contributing to people's lives. I am always wishing I could teach them religion. But it is very difficult. I do not have the qualification."

She currently pays for a few relatives' children's full schooling, particularly the children who have lost their parents; she just finished putting one niece through university. She contributes to many others in the various basic ways that they desperately need help. For anyone who asks, she stretches herself to do what she can. The village she comes from in the Southern Philippines is poor. Every year it is hit by some act of nature, usually a hurricane, and all crops are wasted. There is never a shortage of opportunity to extend help, whether material, emotional, or spiritual.

In the context of material deprivation and insecurity, sometimes people tell her she should focus more on material gain. She explains, "I do that [helping others] because I had the same experience as these children. So, I can't help it." Statistics show that most people who experience ill treatment in childhood continue doing the same to others in adulthood, whether it is abuse or miserliness. Although they know that they did not like what happened and actually do not want to do the same, they end up mimicking the same behavior. Her awareness comes from having developed a higher consciousness about her experience. She shares, "I am taking care of family and extended family always. Sometimes I would be beaten as a child, like if I simply broke a glass. Things like this taught me it's painful, to never treat people that way."

The success she defines for herself, therefore, is not at the material level. Success means much more. A higher notion of success is gained through recognizing the Divine in others and the right to dignity and help. Through this higher perspective from experience of childhood struggle, her actions are given greater meaning. She further explains, "I feel happy when I help other people. I am proud if I help other people. My sister told me I am doing wrong when she found out I helped the girl through schooling. But I am happy for this girl because for me money is nothing but to make people happy. I am even happier than they are." She stresses, "If I give to other people, God gives me what I need. If you give to other people, I believe God gives you double. I tell others to give, who tell me not to give."

"People think I'm successful. Everyone who put me down before and harmed me comes now and asks for help because they can't believe that I have survived," Rowena laughs. She further explains that often people focus only on money and material gain. She tells me a stepbrother who is relatively wealthy came to the conclusion recently that through her example money isn't the greatest thing to have. He told her that even though he has money, she is ahead in life. He apologized to her for not helping her during childhood. She affirms the best advice she could give him in response was, "Just have faith in God and trust in the One God, then you will have. You might have money, but you do not have faith. You must have faith."

~

## ☙ 18 ❧

# A Mission for Peace After War: Bosnia and Serbia

*"In war you are blind, you start to see. At the end of war you see. People who gained seeing look at grass and say, how beautiful."*

## Introduction

Some months ago I had the opportunity to visit Bosnia. Bosnians explained how their country is called the land of blood and honey (which is also the title of the 2011 film *In the Land of Blood and Honey*). The most recent spate of violence in the heart of this beautiful land was the Bosnian War that took place in Bosnia and Herzegovina officially dated between March 1992 and December 1995. The factions in the war were forces within Bosnia and Herzegovina, Bosnian Serbs, Bosnian Croat, and Bosnian Muslims. It should be noted, however, that the Balkans have been viewed as high geopolitical value to Western powers. Therefore, this war is waged in that context and is not merely Serb initiated genocide.

To provide context, in Bundestag, Hans-Dietrich Genscher, then foreign minister in Bonn, Germany, announced his support for the separation of the six

Balkan states. This was for revenge against Serbs for their help in defeating Germany/Austria during the First World War. As will be teased out in a later discussion on Iraq and the Middle Eastern region, this policy of Balkanization or division is intended to weaken potentially strong groups in a strategically important area. The focal target was the Serbs. Although Britain, France, and the U.S. would have otherwise welcomed this proposal, it was viewed, being stated by Germany, as out of step, and Genscher was dismissed later and Gerhard Stoltenberg, shortly as minister of defense, fired. Nonetheless, Stoltenberg had six shiploads of weapons sent to Turkey. Germany also gave Montenegro the Deutsche Mark—to provoke Serbia.

Slobodan Milošević had suggested that all groups be united on the model of Switzerland. Further, to the chagrin of the U.S., Russia supported the idea. Croatians and Slovenians recruited their armies. In 1992, following the Slovenian and Croatian secessions from Yugoslavia in 1991, the three ethnic groups inhabiting Bosnia and Herzegovina, Muslim Bosniaks (44 percent), Orthodox Serbs (31 percent) and Catholic Croats (17 percent) made a referendum for independence. The political representatives of the Bosnian Serbs rejected any idea of unification. Kosovo did not consider separation until that point. Once independence was declared, the Bosnian Serbs, supported by the Serbian Government of Milošević and the Yugoslav People's Army (JNA), mobilized their forces into Bosnia and Herzegovina to secure Serb territory. The Serbs also feared becoming a minority again due to their long history of displacement and being massacred, losing 27 percent of the Serb population in World War I and the genocide of 500,000 Serbs in World War II. Now, this event began the largest conflict in Europe since World War II.

The war was characterized by indiscriminate shelling of cities and towns, ethnic cleansing of the Bosniak people and systematic mass rape, mostly by Serb forces with 90 percent, according to a CIA report,[15] and to a lesser extent Croat forces. Between 100,000 and 110,000 people were killed[16] and 2.2 million displaced. As of 2008, forty-five Serbs, twelve Croats and four Bosniaks were convicted of war crimes.[17] I was told that many more are still walking the streets who were also directly responsible for acts of genocide and crimes against humanity.

I had visited Bosnia earlier in the year before the war had officially started, as part of an unplanned trip. For being barely twenty at the time and coming from a very isolated part of the very north of Canada, the little I saw was entirely surreal. Upon my return a few decades later, I stood on top of the hill in Sarajevo in the cool rain looking out into the land of blood and honey. On the lush green hills, close and distant, were scattered masses of graves where mostly young men died and were buried on the spot. I thought to myself, these young men were alive as I came through earlier and some were younger than I was.

Mirza Sarajkic, who stood beside me, provided more details. Picturing those details before me where a patch of grave stones were erected, I then narrowly flashed back with my memory of my own little taste of hiding from a group of drunken soldiers firing their guns literally indiscriminately, among the trail of events. At the time, two Serb families, glimpsing two displaced foreigners, my friend and myself, came out and pulled us into their place. Exclaiming shock at us two young women on the street, they imparted how lucky we were to be alive, something which we were not thinking about but made complete sense. Now standing on the hill, Mirza shifted his account from wisdom to one of acceptance. He fought on the front lines at the age of fourteen and is lucky to live to talk about it. He saw everything firsthand. Yet, what I noticed is that he remained grounded and serene, not allowing himself to finish before offering compassionate insights. I realized quickly he had embodied the violence, its traumas, and most significantly the transformation.

This account is one of successfully transforming the self through extremes of experiences to then find life purpose. Mirza's is a mission for peace. In his example, transformation can in fact lead to great success as a spiritual activist in spite of and because of such extremes in life experiences.

## Is There a Point to Suffering?

The atrocities were unfathomable. During the war, I had participated in an organization that helped those who escaped and would later apply for refugee status. These people included a few Serb families, but the vast majority were Bosniaks. We coordinated efforts to gather the most basic items and gave them to displaced individuals and those who, often within 48 hours, had just made dramatic escapes. All were desperate and some had not had access to basic amenities and food for a long period of time; they could not believe they were in such a position to accept things such as toothbrushes, soap, shampoo, and clothing.

Some had seen brothers and fathers marched off (who they would never again see). Among other things done to them, they had rifles jammed down their throats or into their heads to keep their eyes open to watch fathers and brothers tortured to death just feet in front of them. A systematic means of warfare aimed to reach new levels of psychological trauma and wounding was to have torture and rape watched. Exhausted, raw with pain, and still in utter disbelief, they told it like it was.

How can a human being have any desire for life when suffering can be so immense? Anyone who has lived through a great ordeal may wonder if there is any purpose for the pain. Sometimes it seems there is no point. It is understandable then that not everyone who comes out of a situation of war surpasses bitterness. Not one person I spoke to on this last trip in Sarajevo, had not lost a family member, relative, friend, or colleague in this war. I heard numerous stories about bitterness, hate, continued denial of responsibility, and unforgiveness. One person who lived under the siege in Sarajevo exclaimed that he wished NATO had not sent the little food because the deaths around him were, in his eyes, orchestrated to be slow. He came out deeply wounded and angry that those he loved died a painful death and, as he describes, he was on life support to watch it.

Mirza had lost several relatives during the war and during its burning his family had been expelled from their village and homes. "War is such a state of being. If you have 10 percent of security you realize that life is so precious. You come to know that every human's life is so precious. . . . Every day is gambling, being alive or not." His coming from the middle of this disaster, fighting on the front lines as a fourteen-year-old, confinement within the siege in the village of Prijedor where his family and most of his relatives lived, and continuing to pick up the pieces for lives shattered gave rise to this expanded awareness. Mirza tells of his personal experience,

Where you see thousands killed and beaten to death. Family members were in that one huge detention death camp. They were there for between one to three and a half years. I saw the darker side of human beings, what they are able to do. First I felt helplessness and lost all senses for everything. I could not believe what was happening, that neighbours could do those atrocities. They could exterminate all of us.

However, his experience merely gave rise to his ability to access spiritual intelligence and use an expanded knowing to search for meaning and purpose. Not everyone learns to perceive meaning. Most people choose only to see the suffering. Suffering is not the same as pain; it is always meaningless.

Beyond hearing the numerous firsthand accounts, one can watch the faces of passers-bye in the city of Sarajevo in an attempt to know and feel what lies in their memories and hearts. It becomes apparent that the entire aura of the city has much healing ahead. Only the actions of people with the help of God's angels will be able to move and transmute such energy. Mirza matter-of-factly shares, "They could only kill us physically. They could not kill the memory of Bosniaks. We may be tortured people for centuries, but we are determined to stay and promote good things."

To transform means to be the very channel through which our spirit is grounded into the reality of dark and light. We can transmute the worst of experiences of pain and loss to acceptance, forgiveness, greater spiritual intelligence, and the success we actually need. The key to surviving and, therefore, succeeding is to grasp its meaning by embracing its purpose for our path.

## A Second Chance

Such lived experience cannot be forgotten and no one can expect such memories to be erased. Yet, despite this heavy collective consciousness his face is one of those which radiates something from within and explains how the experience of war is what helped push a resolve in his life to "stay and promote good things."

> Now, I wake up and thank Mother Nature for life. At fourteen or fifteen, I asked myself 'What is the value of all the things I have in life? Did they make me happy? No.' In war you are blind, you start to see. At the end of war you see. People who gained seeing look at grass and say, how beautiful. Before they did not. When you are out of the war and have freedom to sleep or to travel, it is heaven on earth. After war I got a second chance.

It is this second chance we are given and some of us recognize. It is there "to promote good things." Many deny themselves access to the wisdom of the soul. Not everyone takes the opportunity. When you only see pain in your life circumstances, you miss the opportunity to recognize the higher meaning. Such people close themselves off and continue to suffer.

Those who yearn to expand through it "start to see." This "second chance" is prompting you to choose the higher road of being and action. It is an opportunity and a blessing. Nothing is random. The pain may be so immense but your soul co-creating with its Lord knows that such an experience is the best way for you to grow and express yourself. In fact, pain is a part of life that exists in order to show us how we can emerge on the other side where there is light to have and to share. Perhaps Mirza did want out at some point, too. But he has a deep and compelling knowing that he, both of himself and collectively, must "stay" to complete what he is called for.

We all have tasks to complete before we leave. We must be in communion with the earth plane, with the material challenges and opportunities in which we find ourselves. It is, however, totally up to us to choose to learn. Your soul cannot force you. You must choose. You can choose a space of bitterness, hopelessness, and further hurt. You can choose to accept the gifts of wisdom that your experience is extending to you. Like many others in the region, Mirza has great opportunity to spread light today because the darkness has been so vast and encompassing.

## Finding Purpose

Mirza's question is so significant to each of us: "What is the value of all the things I have in life? Did they make me happy?" I have one friend, educated and professional, who has, beyond her lounging clothing, only four full outfits that she mixes and matches—no more. She is not without tests. I was just speaking to her yesterday and she is a reminder for me that for all the challenges I have had in life I must be humbled and grateful because hers are extreme and I may not be able to endure what she is enduring right now. But her one approach to life is among others in which she puts emphasis in all her actions to bringing joy to others, not to accumulating, just having enough to be comfortable and extending herself to put love in so many lives.

But the vast, vast majority of us are missing the point of living and the meaning of success. Our neighbour has a new car; we must do better. There is a new fashion; we must keep up with it. A new phone is out; we need it. We work harder to accumulate more. What are we doing if we run over grass to get to somewhere and not feel the grass beneath our feet? Yes, prices are rising but it is because we are part of a system of consumption that we are feeding back into, too. We believe in it and act on it. In this vicious cycle of taking we forget about those who need. We are being distracted from what is really going on in our world—the Congo, Tibet, Somalia, and so on. We are missing the point of life; we are missing our calling if we are in the vicious cycle of working to accumulate more than we need.

Mirza's struggle is not dissimilar to that of Rowena's, illustrated earlier. Although their struggles are within completely different contexts, their realization of life purpose and meaning to life converge. Their struggles remind me that goals in life are simple. When we can live with such wisdom, success is inevitable. His goals may not seem grand; yet, they are profoundly purposeful. He has learned to love God's creations as simple as the grass. He adds, "I want to know people. It is important for me. I want to make people smile, to have more smiley faces on the street. I don't like heated discussions or arguments." These actions are, however, the basics that keep a person going, surviving and often able to reach greater heights of happiness, love, and inspiration. In working towards offering such basic necessities, he adds, " . . . I try to find the best way to serve humanity." In taking such steps, he is able to move to the grand scale, to arguably more complicated steps, because in serving humanity he must transform his pain to love. To come from the depths of despair and loss and give to not only your community, but also your enemy is beyond grand. It is truly transformative.

Spiritual activism is most simply accessing wisdom from life's tests and calamities and using these to bring light into the places that need it. It is unique because our experiences are unique. For Mirza, it means continuing to fight for justice by taking steps to convict those responsible for acts against humanity in his village and against his relatives. He is a university lecturer and a poet. Yet, his energy is not exhausted because he remains practical with his goals to create change using further means. He participates with three charities and although detests confrontation, regularly engages in meetings to work towards justice. And while he calls attention to the atrocities that have not had thorough investigation, he works to mend relations between Bosniaks and Serbs by participating in further faith-based organizations and activities that bring Bosniaks, Serbs, and Croats together to find common ground in faith. When asked if he feels any enmity, he answers, "I see pain in the faces of Bosniaks, but I actually see more pain in the faces of Serbs. In some way, I think it is easier for us to overcome what happened if we want to but it seems harder for Serbs. They are still living in the pain. No, I feel sorry for them."

*Faith, Purification, Love, Wholeness*
Wondering if grave challenges, such as war or immense sense of loss, are the critical ingredient for spiritual

activism, I pushed Mirza to tell me if that assumption was true. For him, war definitely made him "change direction in life," as he put it. But he adds that most important is the development of critical practices. These can be awakened through such experience but need not be. He says that his upbringing was also important. His role model is his mother who was also an activist and what he describes as a "fighter" under the Communist regime. Mirza then stressed what he called a third variable for his inspiration for creating change: faith. He told of another critical point early on that reopened connection.

> I heard a professor praying downstairs. At that moment I was celebrating my good grades. I was eighteen years old and just finished high school. At that time I had no communication with my Lord. I simply decided to pray, too. Still I was arrogant while in the middle of my prayer. I told Him that I wanted to go to Hajj [pilgrimage], to the Kaaba [the sacred place of Muslim pilgrimage made at least once in a lifetime to Mecca]. I was blackmailing God.

> So, I went when I was twenty. It was as I was going that I actually remembered that I had asked to go a few years before. I realized that my number one dream came true and very easily. This was a major lesson for me. People do not believe. But the amount of energy I got when my dream came true was immense. It urged me to convince people that dreams can come true. That is why I am a person today who can be in three places at the same time.

Connection and service to God is a critical ingredient we all have. While pain is a gift and opportunity and early childhood examples of strength are there for some, we can all access higher wisdom, our soul wisdom, to perceive our purpose and embrace our person with action.

Accessing our soul and the Divine does help guide us. It simultaneously provides us with the power and energy we need to fulfill our purpose. Our soul and the higher realms are multi-dimensional; spirit and soul are Light energy. Connection with Spirit, those from beyond and God's creations, is the key to nurturing and sustaining activism. At a later time I asked Mirza to elaborate on how he sustains himself and works with connection. He says,

> I just returned from one of the places that inspires me. It elevates the spirit in me. I went to the area of Srebrenica and Zvornik, places that went through severe massacres and genocide during the last war. I use to spend Eid (a major Muslim religious festivity) there. There is neither Internet nor mobile connection. . . .Watching the people there, listening to their stories, feeling their strength, to come back to the places where their beloved ones were literally slaughtered, raped, and massacred . . . these people, their life stories and way of living touches the deepest inside of me.

> To eat with them, to participate in daily activities, going to the well, taking care of the cattle and sheep, collecting the forest fruits, visit the graveyard and be silent in front of the tombs and mass graves . . . all of this is like a Divine poem and melody. That leaves indelible traces in the soul and mind. To pray with them at the emerald green meadows, to sing their sad songs in the sunset time, all of this

is a unique event, almost surreal. If you add to this the awareness, the strength and will of all the people that come back to visit the place of death, an erased world they used to have . . . speechless. . . .

Another key is purification. Accessing Light purifies. The darkness of the war must be cleansed. Mirza and the many others that have overcome a great deal to make the trip to the country villages to be together with those living and those who are in spirit are engaging in spiritual acts of transmutation. If they do not actively do this, Mother Earth will and when she does her forces work swiftly and often completely. The darkness must be alchemized at some time and therefore for these people to take on the task they must face and experience indescribable pain, pain which Mirza cannot fully articulate in any real way but as "speechless." The acts these wonderful people are engaged in enable them to open their hearts and receive. In doing this, they are cleansing and expanding. They are purging and filling the soul.

These people are working with energies that humans and Earth are connected with, both light and dark. They are true emissaries of Light on the physical plane because they have courageously taken on the responsibility to bring this Light into the Earth as allies to humans and Earth. Yet, they comprise few who have actually accepted their soul calling for transmutation and healing. If only more people knew the incredible value of transmutation of pain to peace through being with All That Is in the way these people do, our world's consciousness would be healed.

While there I visited the foot of a mountain from which a fast river gushes forth. It comes literally out of a mountain, runs for a few miles and then disappears again into the earth. The cold mineral-rich river brings many searching for connection to the place for reflection, contemplation, and prayer. Mirza told me of another place he visits for connection where he spends hours at the top of the mountain of Bjelasnica, more than 2,000 meters high. He was reluctant to explain his sacred and intimate moments, but I really wanted to know how he gains the sustenance he radiates in his being and actions. He describes his trips to Bjelasnica, "In that vast space, true revelation of God, untouched nature, the Lord is so close; His signs overflow the mind and the earth. You realize how small you are, but at the same time how Divine you are with Him. And so then you come to know why it is you yearn for Him."

Transmutation of the remnants of darkness is organic when one opens his heart to reflect the Divine light and enable it to shine through the soul. Activists tend to forget just how significant the process of healing the self is to the healing of the earth in practice. Mirza continues explaining the significance of time with Source,

> Qijamu layl, the prayer in the last third of night [towards the end of the Muslim month of fasting, Ramadan] is more than elevating. The reading Qur'an, or engaging in an interview (muqabala) with Allah, polishing the crumbs and remnants of the soul in His mirror, all of this is a healing experience. Sometimes a blink of this experience appears during daily prayers, although rarely.

Mirza's experience with connection reveals that connection is love and being love at all times and throughout our day. It should not be arrived at in quiet contemplation on top of a mountain or in seclusion and then left behind; it must be engaged in all our dealings and it is in such dealings that the Divine comes forth and heals in practice. For him, connection is lived when,

> Listening to my wife, Emina's recitation of Qur'an, Emina's splendor in her eyes when looking at me, my mother's hug and gaze during our farewells, my father's sadness when leaving his grandson, and my son, Hamza . . . all of these are bits of a huge and amazing spiritual puzzle that Allah bestows upon me, from time to time, when this heart of mine is clear enough to see and hear signs dancing around me, dancing around all of us.

We need not experience the depths of pain to see, although our souls often choose such means. By opening our hearts to the Divine we can also be emissaries of Light and love, healing the many aspects of ourselves and our world that need the Divine light. By keeping our hearts open we bridge the distance between heaven and earth. Such examples shows us the simple goals of bringing happiness, love, and peace are indeed the grand goals that we need to achieve together.

∽

# ⚘ 19 ⚘

# Terrorism and Countering Misinformation: Iraq as Starting Point

*"I simply refuse to obey because it is against my intuition and my conscience. This is not right. I value my inner belief of what is right and wrong."*

## Introduction

Imad Khadduri has spent the last decade countering a misinformation campaign, primarily concerning the nuclear program in Iraq. He talks to me about how misinformation and the resultant strategic actions taken by the super powers have resulted, among many things, in millions of deaths. Iraq is only the starting point. The same can be said for Iran. In any case, he reveals his struggle and the challenges ahead that should concern anyone interested in how misinformation and, thereby ensuing actions, have produced terrorism and will continue to do so, unless large scale activism to counter such strategy is seen.

When Khadduri stood up to Saddam Hussein, he and his family barely escaped from Iraq alive. He earned a PhD in Nuclear Reactor Technology and worked with the Iraqi Atomic Energy Commission from 1968 to 1998. He has been interviewed by numerous networks on his knowledge of the Iraqi and Iranian nuclear programs. He now uses all opportunities through media and his books to launch awareness and put it into action. As he tells me, "After Occupy Wall Street—people were made more aware. But awareness is like breathing air. You cannot eat it." The key he identifies to creating change is moving from an opportunist calculation of self interest and of a pure technological basis for action to broader thinking and importantly action, one which includes values, principles, and conscience of right and wrong.

## Geopolitics and Identity

Geopolitics that have caused Balkanization and the resultant wars between groups living otherwise peacefully or potentially peacefully, has been applied the same way to the Middle Eastern region all the way to Afghanistan. The results are similar. Both U.S. and Russian powers, among earlier European powers, have well understood the resource value and political value of controlling these regions for a very long time and now even more so. What this means is that because this whole strip from the Balkans, down the Arab Gulf, Iraq included, to Afghanistan is of critical strategic importance to self-interested economic and political goals, as part of a military strategy it is rationalized as important to conquer, occupy, and divide. As Khaddurri explains, "It is not about democracy." Democratic values and principles are not in the equation for geopolitics.

Khadduri also points out that to address such a situation, identity is crucial. When identity is strong in terms of knowing who you are, you are grounded and committed. Khadduri explains that what drives him to action is commitment, "It is a sense of commitment which is engraved in my conscience by being an Arab, an Iraqi Arab, a Christian Iraqi Arab. It instills what I was raised with as a child because they are influenced by their parents, their Arab Christian culture and which they transferred to me when I was young." But he also explains that identity must be broader. He continues, "At the same time I mingled with other Iraqi Muslims and Jews," and points out how programs of misinformation have caused the deterioration of this broad cultural identity. He adds that education, too, is a pillar of the culture and is essential as part and parcel of strengthening identity and gaining knowledge.

He explains, therefore, that he conceptually understood the politics of identity through reading Karl Marx's capitalist estrangement of man from his inner self resulting in materialist thinking and the development of capitalism, and especially through Erik Fromm and his discussion on the role and effect of cultural alienation in the early 60s when he went to study in the U.S. In fact, he says this growing awareness of Self through what he learned prompted him to decide that he would only marry an Iraqi and raise his children with his Iraqi familial values. Through this experience, he attests, "Even at the young age of twenty-one I learned to value how bountiful my Iraqi culture is and especially my Iraqi Christian culture."

Khadduri has hit a pivotal key to enabling a just world. If one does not know himself at the core of his being and trust who he is and cooperate with others with this respect for an inner sacred Self, then one cannot grasp values and principles that come from knowing oneself. I asked him if he could possibly see himself with a global identity to which he countered that identity must and can only start with who you really are from your own cultural milieu, and points out how various cultures have been assimilated and destroyed due to the inability to hold onto something more tangible and self-confirming, usually resulting in physical death and destruction. Indeed, he is correct. In our drive for global peace, we forget that identity is always embedded in political structures and hierarchy. It has therefore been used as core strategy in geopolitics to ensure groups are so weakened, not merely militarily, but significantly in the ability to assert a Self that can cooperate with other Selves to then protect wider dignity, freedom, and rights.

## How Misinformation Works

As a modern form of a somewhat Machiavellian way of thinking, a particular mentality extends itself through "information," directives, and the making of laws. This approach to politics importantly includes the support of citizens. But, through such mechanisms, citizens uphold whatever it desires because the information they receive usually works to create the same desires. Khadduri names more accurately the neoconservatives as those who began extending the machinery of information to guide support for invasion into Iraq. He describes how they believed they were entitled to rule over humanity through misinformation due to might. Khadduri speaks specifically of the misinformation campaign in Iraq as built on falsehood and lies, coordinated by the government and corporate media, as undermining principled choices and action. The same is applied to Iran. He explains, however, that such misinformation campaigns are not that simplistic. He tells how Iran, meanwhile, has also played a pivotal role in this campaign.

Khadduri had visited every single nuclear scientist and nuclear engineer while setting up his network across Iraq. Leading up to the Iraq invasion in 2003, Khadduri was asked by numerous journalists and networks to comment on the nuclear weapons program that Collin Powell falsely claimed was still in existence. As he explains, sometimes journalists were bold in quoting some of what he said accurately. But very often he was sidelined because his account did not support the goal to invade. The wealth of information he gave providing evidence that the program had ended was often never put into print. Media, thus, serves as the arm of this Machiavellian approach.

At the government level, much had been said to the public that was simply untrue. Powell claimed that Iraqi scientists had to sign that they would face a death penalty if they revealed secrets to the IAEA inspection team. But Khadduri was one of those scientists and they all in fact had to sign at least four agreements that if they did not give over everything in their possession to the IAEA they would face death. Powell claimed there were buildings and infrastructure for the program, but as Khadduri well remembers because many of his colleagues and their families housed closeby had been killed when they were all bombed out—they were long destroyed since the 80s. They no longer existed after 1991. With all sorts of documents used as evidence proven false and all sorts of lies proven erroneous, and then even with IAEA's Mohamed el-Baradei's conclusion that Iraq did not rejuvenate a nuclear weapons program, Vice President Cheney claimed el-Baradei was wrong and U.S. Intelligence had proof that the program existed.

While the public did not have to know about the geopolitical significance of destroying Iraq's infrastructure and identity, it was repeatedly reminded of the American way of life needing to be protected. And that is what Khadduri points to as the level of rational linear thinking and desire that works to create support along with misinformation. As Khadduri describes, people can agree to protect their American way of life without needing to know much more. However, because of such narrow thinking and misguided action, Khadduri fears, global terrorism will grow exponentially.

*Iraq, Iran, and the Future of Terrorism*

Khadurri tells me that once every two or three years a person would commit suicide in Iraq. He says, "It's against the culture; it's unheard of because there is a social net. There is first the family, then the friends, then the tribe, then the school friends—nobody allows you to commit suicide. They are there to help you solve these very existential problems." He explains,

So, when the suicide bombers came to attack the American soldiers, I had to ask what is motivating them? My first impression was the occupation so fractured and damaged the identity, the cultural cohesiveness of the Iraqis, especially the young. The weaponry of the Americans is so overwhelming that these young people came to the conclusion that the only weapon they can have against the American soldiers is themselves, blowing themselves up in the midst of the American soldiers. Starting 2004 every week we saw suicide bombing. I decided to investigate this.

What will terrorism look like in the future? What is Iran's role? Although Iran is accused of developing nuclear capacity for military purposes, mainly by the U.S., Khadduri describes it has a role in the deterioration of Iraq, Syria, and the entire surrounding region that is in line with U.S. geopolitical strategy. He tells me,

Khomeini came to power and with him this *wilayat al faqih* [guardianship of the jurist in Shia political and religious thought]. . . . He introduced his thinking of *wilayat al faqih* in the Iranian constitution. When he came in 1979 I didn't think much of it. Then we started to see in the universities women starting to wear the veil; we made fun of them in the 80s. But it grew and grew and grew and the whole thing blossomed into a real sectarian divide. Now I see how divisive, corrosive, and damaging that is and this makes me very fearful. It will, indeed, shed a lot of blood. And we have not had our Protestant revolution. Islam has not had its Protestant upheaval. They did, the *Mu 'tazilah* [movement in Basra and Baghdad based on reason] ten centuries ago and they were supressed. And since that time, the rule of submission to a religious Imam, or the *Khamenei*, or the *Ikhwan al Muslimeen* [Muslim Brotherhood], that is the fundamental pillar on which they stand. They submit, not revolt. This is a historical epoch. I only wish that the Muslims will revolt against that, but at the moment the road until that is a lot of bloodshed.

In other words, the future of terrorism, as Khadduri sees it, will get worse given the trajectory we are on before there can be hope that it can get better. And his prediction of what will likely happen has proved true beyond the daily acts of violence in Iraq. The revolts and their brutal and bloody crushing in Egypt in July and August 2013 began with a coup on the Muslim Brotherhood government. Citizens there and in the region asked for religious-based rulers to go and Muslim Brotherhood supporters see the military coup in Egypt as part of illegal power grabbing. Further on Iraq, Khadduri comments, "Until the 80s there was no sectarianism. I didn't know if my friends were Shia or Muslim until any died. I never asked them. . . . I am shocked in the past few years of the great crack in the Arab society because of this sectarian divide. There is so much wealth of cultural embrace that I am still hopeful that the Arabs, at least Arabs, will be able to overcome this sectarian Grand Canyon that is opening up in front of them."

But, is Iran developing nuclear weapons? That is what the U.S. has claimed after Iraq. In discussing misinformation and the complexity of political strategy, Khadduri draws my attention to al Qaida: "They started killing the resistance in 2006. Why are they fighting the resistance? I started thinking—Good Lord—this is beyond me. I have to start to understand al Qaida's mentality. It all gelled with Iran's nuclear program. The al Qaida thinking, the *wilayat al faqih* thinking and now the nuclear program."

Khadduri describes,

Since I was in charge of the Iranian nuclear program monitoring since 1974 in Iraq—I was tasked to write a monthly report on what Iran was doing. All the indications, scientifically speaking, were pointing to them making an atomic bomb. They were going the plutonium pathway, the uranium enrichment, they are playing all the cards, they made use of our failure, and so forth. Then suddenly, last year, I was in Manama, Bahrain, passing through and I read . . . in a book . . . that in the 60s when Khomeini was still in Qom, they were discussing *Fiqh* [from the theocratic point of view of Islam], 'Is a nuclear weapon allowed? Can it be used?' Various *Ayatollahs* [title given to top twelve shia clerics] had various opinions. I began to see the agenda points that are agreed upon by the 5 plus 1 negotiating with Iran during the IEEE talks. I went and dug. . . .

Go back in 1958—we were part of the Baghdad Pact. The U.S. sent us the atomic energy library. I found the books on the Manhattan project. We imitated the Manhattan project to get our bomb, they sent a 0 power reactor as a gift when the revolution took place. I said, let's give it to the Shah. . . . So, it was taken off to Iran. In 1967 Iran bought a research reactor for the University of Tehran from Brazil. And the fuel was 20 percent enriched. It is still there. For me it's a prime mover of all Iranian policy. In 1967 until the 1990s the fuel that they sent at the time was being exhausted. That reactor was used primarily for research and primarily to produce medical isotopes for cancer treatment. They wanted another 20 percent. America said 'No.' Iran said, 'Okay', and they started another enrichment.

Beginning in the 1990s, they had uranium. The Pakistani Khan gave them the centrifuges. And they kept after asking for the 20 percent.

In 2010, Iran through Turkey made a deal with Brazil. They said, 'We have enriched uranium, now. We will give you 1200 kilos of 5 percent enriched; give us 150 kilos 20 percent enriched'. . . .Turkey was the negotiator. It took months . . . it was ready to be signed and America said 'No way.' So, Iran said, ' . . . we are going to do it.' So, they went from 5 percent to 20 percent. And technologically they managed to build the cladding, which holds the uranium inside, which is very difficult technology.

But in the meantime, since 1995, they started building their own heavy water reactor, which is natural uranium. It doesn't need any enrichment . . . heavy water is very difficult to get. So, they built a whole plant in the middle of Iran for heavy water. . . . And they designed their own natural uranium, forty mega watts.

When we knew about this a decade ago, we thought—'Good Lord—what do they want this for?' Plutonium—that means it's going to be a bomb. They have a uranium bomb and plutonium bomb. It's as clear as the sun. . . .

Here's what transpired. Then in 2012, Khamenei issued a *fatwa* [legal opinion or ruling]—it's illegal to use nuclear weapons. The 5 plus 1 negotiations took place after Khamenei spoke. It hit me—fifty years later they issued this *fatwa*? After that meeting in Kazakhstan I dug further and lo and behold the

Iranians said to the Americans 'Look you're worried about this heavy water plutonium—we have done this reactor to produce more isotopes for medical purposes. . . . And to get a bomb out of plutonium, you need to have a reprocessing plant to extract the plutonium. We are not going to build a reprocessing plant. . . . Secondly, it's under IEEE inspection.' To produce military plutonium, you need to eradiate the fuel in a short period of time, a few months, and take it out; otherwise, it will be turned into plutonium 240 which is a poison for a bomb. The bomb will explode prematurely. . . .The Iranians said to the Americans, 'Come and see how we are operating the reactor'. . . .The Americans said, 'No.' Finally, they operated the heavy water plant. In 2014, the whole reactor will be online.

It's peaceful. The Iranian program is peaceful. I am convinced they are not up to the bomb. And they even agreed, 20 percent you can have a bomb, but 19.5 percent you can never have a bomb, and they agreed to 19.5. Plus there is Khamenei's *fatwa* that it is illegal under Islam to use the bomb.

Khadduri believes that for all these reasons, technically and religiously, there is no development of a bomb, although he mentions the concept of *taqiya* [dissimulation, double language], taking into consideration whether or not the *fatwa* is sincere. Nonetheless, Khadduri warns of not only misinformation, sanctions, and invasion, but also various other overt strategies will create greater terrorism, first of which is supressing any other form of governance and anyone who is defined as "against us." He recalls how the U.S. said to the Afghans, "Give us bin Laden or we will attack you." He points out that the Afghanis adopted their own democracy in a cultural sense. "They held a meeting with 250 tribal leaders. They met for three days in Afghanistan to discuss the issue. After three days of democratic discussion, the decision was, 'Look America, if you can prove it was him we'll give him to you. But as long as he is our guest in our Bedouin culture, he is protected by us. We won't give him up.' Khadduri laments the millions of deaths ten years later, and comments, "So, this lack of respect for cultural democracy, instead of letting it grow as it did naturally for them will be dangerous."

He points out, too, how terrorism is applied broadly now to people, for example, Edward Snowden, who blew the whistle on NSA spying. With the issue of fracking, he shows that they are even asking for legislation for those who are protesting to be called terrorists. He adds, "They are expanding 'everybody who is not with us is a terrorist' even though they are peaceful protestors. So, people with a conscience are now attacked and labelled as terrorists because they are against the system's economic and political interests. Now," he warns, "people are also moving towards extreme ideologies. Unless a cataclysmic event happens, terrorism will increase."

*Beyond Terrorism*

Going back to role of family influence on him, Khadduri recalls, "My father practiced medicine in a poor area of Baghdad. He often gave services for free to the poor, so he had little money. . . .When he died, he had the equivalent of only 1,000 dollars in his name. People would ask him, 'Why are you so sacrificing?' He would reply, 'Because I am building two castles, Imad and Waleed [Khadduri's brother], stone by stone, and that's all I have in life. Slow building.'" Khadduri explains this is reflected in his dealings with people. He tells me, "There is a saying by Ali, Mohamed's [the prophet's] cousin: '*El Din al muamila* [how you treat/deal with people is my religion].' That's religion. It's how you deal with others. The highest essence of my spiritual practice is what Imam Ali said."

As a result, Khadduri describes how he stood up to authority several times when his conscience would not allow him to do what was asked of him. He says, "I simply refuse to obey because it is against my intuition and my conscience. This is not right. I value my inner belief of what is right and wrong. It's not related to religion. . . . Growing up you know who you are and you stick with it. You don't become an opportunist, you don't become a business cheater. It is through getting to know yourself humbly."

I ask Khadduri to share additional reasons behind the reluctance of most people to forgo opportunism and embrace their conscience when they can do something to stop oppression or control of others. He explains,

One thing is if it doesn't directly affect them; it's not their job, if it's not their next vacation they won't do anything. If you tell them it is something very dangerous, they say, 'Okay, we've got so many other things that are threatening.' And being part of an alienated culture, especially in the West, they don't care about a humanitarian aspect. They label those who are saying something 'activists' and so move on. There is no human dimension to it. Alienation has strong foundations in the West, especially in the States. They don't react because in a sense they are alienated from their human dimension.

Khadduri still says he is optimistic. He tells me, "I believe so much in my culture and history to be optimistic." But what he adds is echoed by others who study issues of world peace and politics using more than rational linear atomistic thinking, and by those who work with the key of spiritual intelligence. He adds, "But it will not be in my generation or my son's; three or four generations from now. Our culture will absorb these aberrations. I don't give up."

~

# ⁓ 20 ⁓

# Transformation: The Arab Spring and Beyond

*"True transformation can only come from the roots of society. Transformation occurs through learning ethics, transparency and right conduct in every field. These must happen within the institutions of learning."*

## Introduction

The Arab Spring started in Tunisia and spread quickly to Egypt, Libya, Yemen, Syria, and all surrounding countries. There are many discussions on the reasons for the Arab Spring. Being in Egypt during parts of the Arab Spring, and interviewing and researching numerous individuals, men and women, in the decade leading up to the overthrow of the Mubarak regime after its thirty-year rule, it is clear that the huge and ever growing disparity between the haves and have-nots is the pivotal reason. It is the same reason people in Iceland, Hungary, major cities in the U.S., Toronto, and various other places formed Occupy Movements.

These movements will go beyond the Arab Spring and Occupy movements globally. They will show a resurgence, become stronger, and individuals will continue their missions for greater equality for no other reason than the fact that this very disparity between the richer and poorer countries is increasing as well as between the rich and poor in the U.S. How communities and governments respond will be pivotal. What choices they make to share power, wealth, knowledge, and ensure well-being, dignity, justice, and freedom will tell what their—and our collective—future will be like. How individuals seek to find sustainable means to ensure greater civility between themselves, their communities and with government is, nevertheless, crucial. At the same time, Egypt, being the most volumous country in the Middle East and the epicentre of various industries and learning for well over a century and in earlier times, will determine much of this fate. What happens there will have a significant ripple effect. All the while, its future is gravely uncertain.

Mohamed abu Zahra's story is no less typical than many others who have struggled for freedom and justice. Yet, his illustrates the context for his spiritual activism, the meandering path of "spiritual" activism as individuals attempt to grasp illusive solutions, his dreams that keep him pressing forward, and how he struggles for a better future. The keys he uses will be important for others looking for what all these movements have been standing for, in principle: finding purpose. His road has transformed into faith in the Divine. Egypt's collective may go through more trials for a while to come. However, activists, like Mohamed, illustrate the experiences that can be used to shape the Self, enable greater wisdom and, therefore, the keys that will work if enough individuals use them—wherever they are.

## In Tahrir Square

Mohamed played a leading role, among several other individuals, in organizing and motivating individuals in the overthrow of the Mubarak regime. He took part in the organization of hundreds of activists, gathering them and inspiring them to participate in protests in Tahrir Square. With the hundreds of activists that he motivated, Mohamed spent days and nights in the large square in downtown Cairo where the protests began in January 2011. He spent several months in that square, sleeping on the ground in tents, making flyers, and eventually participating in battle. Government forces attacked protestors, crushed them with vehicles, shot at them, and on the day of the Battle of the Camel the protestors met a heavy blow when men on their camels came through the square literally butchering anyone in their way. Mohamed tells me, "We were there for freedom. We have endured the repression of the regime for too long. People were becoming too desperate. Their economic burdens were too great. We were all tired."

The government had paid expert camel riders to do their work on that fateful day. I asked a few of the camel riders what had happened. Two of these men explained that they actually did not know what they were being set up to do. They are from groups that do various types of work. Government officials knew where to find them. They are poor and known as thugs. They grew up on the streets. They were paid and taken to the square where they were told those were bad guys and to finish them off. No one could ride camels as adroitly as they. Mohamed talks about how they were so shocked that they could not react immediately.

Mohamed, of course, was there on that day. He and others I spoke to told how they stayed the entire day throwing back the heavy rocks. They were not rocks. The government-hired forces had chipped off cement blocks to create rocks. Mohamed, as many others I have now spoken to, was hurt severely. The injured were treated by makeshift hospitals placed in the Square for such events. Even women took part in the battle. He exclaims that he watched a few old women participating. One was throwing the rocks. One old woman was carrying what she picked up in her black long dress (*abaya*) and bringing them to the young men. Women banged against metal wall plates as the battle moved into the night to make it sound as if there were many more protesters than there really were in order to avoid an ambush. Such were actions of endurance, optimism, and hope for a just society and country.

## *Pivotal Point 1: Dealing with an Orphan Label*

Knowing full well that it is often those individuals who endured a hard childhood who learn to take a leading role in the betterment of lives besides their own, I have asked Mohamed to share what motivated him to become interested in fighting for a better Egypt. He names two pivotal experiences he believes are the primary shapers to his activism. The first is being labelled an orphan. He tells me,

> There are personal reasons and public reasons. When I was five years old my dad went to Iraq. That was during the first Iraq war. We didn't hear anything from him. So, we assumed that he was missing.

I started to be an orphan, socially, at least. Society started to sympathize with us. I rejected their sympathy. I tried to especially reject those who tried to assume authority over me. As a result, I became an introvert. I also decided to be successful so that I wouldn't need their sympathy or authority.

So, I memorized the Qur'an at the age of six or seven. My uncle, my mom's brother, was taking care of me. He encouraged me to memorize the Qur'an, so I finished it. My mom was working and taking care of everything. I started reading a lot as a way of becoming self-reliant. I had a strong drive to prove myself in every way.

In the countryside [where Mohamed grew up], the *Ikhwan Al Muslimeen* (Muslim Brotherhood) have the upper hand politically and socially. So, from ten years-old I joined them; I was with the *Ikhwan* youth group. I am thirty, so that was twenty years ago. I started to work with them on cultural and religious projects.

During my summers as a child I worked, which is looked down on by society. But most difficult for me as a child was the problem of charity. People always wanted to give me charity. People would single me out of the class just to give me charity and I would hate it. That was tough, so I would escape from school before the charity distribution time. 'Why not, people are giving you a gift, accept it,' my mother would say. But I would never accept it.

My dad returned when I was in grade nine, when I was fourteen or fifteen. He was away for about ten years. It turned out that he was in prison in Iraq and he returned due to some diplomatic efforts, so he returned totally destroyed financially and health-wise. He needed to recover in the hospital for about six months. My dad's personality is a very authoritarian personality. He wanted to do authoritarian parenthood on us but it was too late; we were already almost out of the nest. At this stage, we had daily arguments, every day, between us. At that time, I was very popular in our society and town through the activism I was in and the loose affiliation I had as a child with the *Ikhwan*.

Mohamed refers to this period of experiencing impoverishment as important for shaping who he is whereby he refused to be labelled as poor and in need of any assistance or charity. He shares that when he went off to university he refused to take any support from his father when he sensed that support would mean that his father would start making decisions for him and instead chose to live on one dollar a week.

## The Arab Spring Consciousness

At university, however, Mohamed's activism increased as he started to take socialist approaches. He worked through the *Ikhwan* for some time as he became more popular in giving courses, yet began to have his own circles of students to train with a socialist approach, different from the *Ikhwan's* ideology. Mohamed was immersed in Marxist literature, which he began when his father returned. He started a newspaper dealing with public issues at college and posted highlights of their concerns everywhere. However, he explains, "People in general did not like these ideas. . . . the ideas of demonstrating against the system—at al Azhar they were abhorred by the students. We started teaching students about materialism theories and other Marxist theories. Other colleagues and groups started to attack us for embracing socialist ideas. Some of us were very extreme about socialism, but I was mostly moderate. I recruited many people during the college and they still hold these ideas today."

In the decades leading up to the Arab Spring, protests were nowhere as visible as in, for example, Latin American or Eastern European countries. Beyond the 1950s with the ousting of the monarchy, the first began with protests around workers' rights, particularly factory workers' rights. Mohamed led the youth in some of these movements after joining a leftist organization. He made these people's hardships and concerns his priority and, in addition, developed a newsletter called *The Workers*, which he and his group distributed to rally the public behind factory workers' rights. Mohamed then began training groups of people in worker's rights and continued to recruit people to the Leftist movement, although his platform was built earlier through his affiliation with the Muslim Brotherhood group.

This activism led to the reviving of the Workers' Party in Egypt. Through these groups, he helped, in fact, organize one of the most well-known protests of the textile factories in Egypt in pre-Arab Spring days. He did not actually feel victorious until he helped organize one around HSBC's project. Mohamed tells of their success. "HSBC was building something huge over the Nile. They took some land owned by people and they blocked two important public roads. So, we encouraged people to demonstrate against HSBC. Of course, security forces attacked us. But the demonstrations continued until the people were compensated and alternative road routes were found. That was a victory for us."

These activities are of no small consequence. In a country in which fighting for rights is met with heavy handed reactions, it is these collective forms of organizing that contributed to a consciousness. This consciousness led to the Arab Spring. It formed the culture of awareness that rights must be fought for and it began in the Workers' movement.

What is so important for success as illustrated in Mohamed's activism is not only that he sparked the idea of protest and the idea that rights are inalienable. He also formed the training courses to enable people to think of choosing freedom and fighting for freedom and rights. Most importantly, he also enabled people to organize themselves and form their own groups. Mohamed explains, "I learned the importance to educate people and let them organize themselves. Let the public demonstrate and take matters into their own hands."

But interestingly, such an approach was not enough for Mohamed. During those years at university, Mohamed says that having immersed himself in materialist theories he doubted the existence of God. He explains,

> Because there is so much injustice, I thought it is impossible there is a God out there. I stared to read about African history and millions of people who died in wars. Most of them died without even knowing why. I believed that the universe was moving at random with no one organizing it. So life was random and injustice is the rule. Every time I fell into a problem, I always felt that suicide was a very possible idea.

## Pivotal Point 2: Uncle's Rejection to Marriage

Mohamed talks about a very low point during his third year at university, which shook him. This is the second point in his life that he identifies as pivotal in questioning values and setting direction as an activist.

> There was a cousin of mine—they live in a different town—who I would see once every year or two or three. We ended up liking each other. Her father, my uncle, is a sheikh in al Azhar, and he would encourage me to be excellent. When I was in third year college, I wanted to be frank with him about my liking his daughter. To make a long story short, I told him, 'I like your daughter and want to marry her after I graduate.' He totally refused that I marry his daughter. He never told me why. My only interpretation was money, and that there was a difference in my academic standing. He thought he could marry his daughter off to some big shot. I was just starting my life off. I was still in the midst and he wanted a stable guy. But I was shocked. I told him, 'What you taught me to value was who I am and not how much I have.' So, I boycotted him. He thought I was impolite. But it was here that I started to ask philosophically why such a thing like this could happen. I knew afterwards that she tried to commit suicide and she tried to escape from home. It was a big drama. So I started to swing towards people's concerns and agonies. At that time, I was ready to be involved in any organization that fights for this cause.

This experience formed the second critical juncture in his life where he determined his life direction and purpose.

> That was such a dark time. I knew I needed something outside of me; I needed to rely on a God. I also started to read critiques of the materialist theories and I started to debate the issues with many people. So, eventually, I started to find a balance between the idea of God and human freedom. And then I started to believe in the Hereafter so that people's mistakes are accounted for and that there would be justice. The idea of justice started to make sense and I started to understand that people who died and who didn't understand God would be blessed and not punished. I started to find a balance, a middle way. I was active with the Leftist movement and their lectures and I was also active with the Islamic movement, the *Ikhwan* and others.

Often the darkest nights are the pivotal points that bring us to search for meaning to life and the Divine to help us through the trial. In this example, Mohamed is ever more determined to share in others' desires and dreams for a better life and fight for shared causes. However, he determined at this juncture that the best way forward was moderation. He explains that his activism from this point on would fully embrace Islamic principles to guide his action.

### Beyond Protest

Two years after the Egyptian revolution in July 2013 the Muslim Brotherhood-led government was pushed by the military to step down. Most assess how the revolution failed to bring a leader to lead the country to a better state. Mohamed's activism took a turn, illustrating the interplay between childhood events, learning, hope, and deep disappointment. The spiritual aspect he hoped to have developed into a socialist system never materialized.

As Mohamed says, "True transformation can only come from the roots of society. Transformation occurs through learning ethics, transparency, and right conduct in every field. These must happen within the institutions of learning." He shuns all group activism, deeply embittered by the larger manifestation at the State level of the *Ikhwan* as a group, whereby freedoms and economic conditions had only been under more strain under the *Ikhwan*-led government. He knows that things often get worse before they get better. He has been in such a place many times before. Each time, he learns to choose a different strategy for activism.

For him, "It must be through reform at the grassroots and, again, through education." Given the changed context, Mohamed directs his energy to teaching media and journalism at Al Azhar university to students he strives to teach with ethics and responsibility. For the time being, he feels that little has been accomplished through group activism. As demonstrated by Egypt's predicament after the Arab Spring, human action is not sufficient. Mohamed also emphasizes that the only way forward is with Divine mercy. He, like many revolutionaries, does not belong to any one side. He is neither Ikhwan nor Liberal. These young revolutionaries found themselves either trying to find new strategies or giving up for the meantime. With the events during the summer of 2013 and the tremendous bloodshed in the streets, mosques and churches, Mohamed decided to do his PhD abroad and return hopefefully better equiped to face an uncertain future.

～

# ≈ 21 ≈

# Geoengineering: A Last Ditch Effort to Save the World?

*"If people stopped looking at how dark the horizon is and started to take action, I think that they would be much more energized and realize that they have tremendous power."*

## Introduction

Stratospheric Aerosol Geoengineering, often referred to as Chemtrails, is the deliberate large-scale injection of sulphur aerosols into the atmosphere. The use of jet airliners is the leading method. Scientists are claiming that these projects are essential to counter polar ice melting caused by global warming and thereby avert a global disaster forecasted for the near future. A massive climate shift is causing imbalances in the ecosystem that have grave consequences on animal and plant life. But the more immediate threat geoengineering is supposedly meant to resolve is methane release from polar ice melting.

There is another set of scientists. They are pointing out that this weather modification—carried out without the awareness or permission of citizens—is actually the primary cause itself for Arctic ice melting and high extinction rates of organisms. They consider it the worst of all types of interventions occurring today. This is not a benign issue. Dane Wigington believes, "it is the greatest untold story of the planet."

Wigington has an extensive background in solar energy. His personal residence was featured in the world's largest renewable energy magazine, *Home Power*. He is the lead researcher for Geoengineering Watch and has investigated geoengineering and HAARP. He assisted Michael Murphy's production, *What in the World Are They Spraying?* and has spoken on numerous channels and networks on the issue of chemtrails and their environmental effects.

Wigington is arguing for the recognition of the interdependence of all life neglected by these programs. He argues that manipulating one aspect of our atmosphere already has dire effects on human organisms and all forms of life. Activism is not something that we take up due to boredom, some fad, or wanting to do something to make us feel good. During my interview with him he asserted that he never saw himself as an activist or politically oriented. Nor did he want to believe that the data he was collecting was true at first. He tells me, "I devoted my life to this only because I feel, based on all available data, that our collective future is literally in the balance with these programs—a sort of nuclear catastrophe I believe that is the greatest threat on the face of the earth." He, therefore, illustrates the most significant dynamic of spiritual activism—action, even for what seems near impossible, is actually vital.

*Effects of Geoengineering*

How do we know that geoengineering is the cause for dramatic changes? There is a recent phenomenon of a massive escalation of metals. As Wigington describes, in California, scientists studying the issue have data on the escalation of metals from CARB (California Air Resources Board). There are geoengineering patents for the processing of artificial ice nucleation. Significantly, from a baseline of aluminium being present to start, within sixty labs in California alone the aluminium count has gone from seven parts per billion up to 34,050 parts. He underscores that this is a 50,000 percent increase in the last ten years. There could be no other cause for this extreme escalation than geoengineering.

Furthermore, we have solar obscuration. Dane did not begin activism around geoengineering until he discovered there was something very wrong on this front. Dane tells me that his home began to lose 60–70 percent of solar uptake from these grid patterns that were being left in the sky. He gathered data and did not even want to believe the data until he did sampling himself. Now, he attests, "The global dimming is 22 percent and that's an unpublicized fact. That is 22 percent of the sun's rays are no longer reaching the surface of the planet."

Dane tells me that trees are dying everywhere in Northern California. Of course, there are many possible causes; however, the link to chemicals being sprayed and tree death, and, more increasingly, the inability to grow produce that once grew easily can no longer be brushed off. In places, such as Northern California, the soil's PH changed up to ten to twelve times more alkaline. The drought conditions are also linked to the massive northern hemisphere hole. Dane tells me that with this situation the bark of trees is literally burning off.

I ask Dane how we can know if there really is a link between these larger than normal lines and grids in the sky and massive changes, including the warming itself. I surmise he deals with this question again and again. We tend to govern ourselves to doubt the most visible technologies of strategy and control. He elucidates,

> We have video footage now of KC 10 KC 135s military tankers spraying on altitudes up close behind the jets, nozzles visible turning on and off. I feel there is no other plausible explanation for this massive amount of metals raining down on us when, one, we have videos of the jet spraying, and, two, we have officials like John Holdren, Obama's science advisor advocating for these programs; as of January 2nd of this year we have a congressional document for the global governance for geoengineering, the metals that are falling on us are the primary ingredients in the patents. It's not coming from China [where heavy concentrations exist but these particulates cannot cross oceans].
>
> It's coming from somewhere. There is no other plausible source given the fact that they are blocking that much of the sun and this stuff is latent in our rain, and, according to geologists, who I spoke to immediately after my first rain sample. One geologist made it clear that there shouldn't be aluminium in our rain where we are unless I live next to a coal factory.
>
> I spoke in front of the California Energy Commission, that is the state energy commission, the largest in the world, and they themselves at that meeting approved the 200,000 dollar spectrometer from Scripts Institute to determine 'the chemical

composition and origin of unknown particulates that were costing the State 20–40 percent of its rainfall.' That's a known consequence of geoengineering. So, even the State of California, who monitors everything, couldn't figure out where these [metals] are coming from.

The State of California is 30 billion dollars in the hole, getting worse each year, being fed back door federal money that's keeping everything afloat—they simply shut up about this. And to take that further, the State stopped testing for aluminium in the water even though they test for everything else under the sun. All the run off tests that go into the tributaries for the Fish and Game Departments and so forth stopped all aluminium testing. The dots just continue to connect.

### Why Are We Being Sprayed?

Among the many reasons conceived for geoengineering are the securing of resources and related security issues and climate control. People are fully aware of how our climate is changing. But it may be quicker than we think. Dane tells me, "They [parts of the U.S. government] are in a panic. Once the Arctic ice cap is gone the albedo is lost. It is already spinning the planet's system out of control." On May 2nd there was an emergency meeting at the White House to address the "Arctic ice death spiral," with scientists pointing out that the arctic ice may be gone within two years. The spraying is increasing because the arctic is melting so rapidly. Dane, in fact, warns that this is connected to these programs and the scale of operation.

Furthermore, with methane in the East Siberian shelf there may be real reason for concern. According to other research, unprecedented plumes of methane have been seen bubbling at the surface of the Arctic Ocean. Dane describes to me that, "the methane alone can and will end life on earth if that entire field releases based on data. The East Siberian shelf alone contains more than enough methane to end life on earth as we know it if it enters the atmosphere."

Spraying was conceived as a way to avert catastrophe. As Dane further explains, the U.S. government is already engaging in Project Lucy, a program to decompose methane in the air using beamed radiofrequency transmissions. In addition, he believes there are now twenty-six ionosphere heaters. They are trying to use opposing frequencies to nuke the atmosphere to degrade the methane in order to halt its spewing off into the atmosphere. They pump it straight into the Arctic. They ice nucleate which is meant to cool the arctic down. But other areas are warming up. For example, in the western U.S., Alaska and Yukon, the weather reached record temperatures in June of 2013. As Dane comments, "It is completely insane, completely without known results. We are able to nucleate the atmosphere and it chemically cools the air but at what cost?" He believes this is a desperate attempt and speculates that other parts of the power structure now realize that the part of their group that was managing the climate has lost all control.

Why would governments do this if they are exposing themselves and citizens to massive levels of toxins? Dane says: "I think for many of the scientists involved, they live in such bubbles and I know some of these people truly believe this is somehow a pharmaceutical cure for planet Earth and I would argue it is a cure that is far worse than the disease." I asked Dane if the pilots are aware of what they are doing. He believes most are not. Commercial planes fitted with the mechanism for spraying are automated and military pilots often have little awareness of why they are flying back and forth. He explains that yet, while some levels of participants may not know what they are participating in and others believe they are working towards saving the planet, they are still contributing to a larger project for resource control and security. In other words, at the highest level of operation, weather control is actually weather weaponry.

What he makes me realize is that the most important first step in activism is the need to ask, "Why"? We inadvertently put power in others' hands, specifically those in authority—and, more accurately, those who have control over authority. We feel empowered by the *idea* that we have freedom of speech, first amendment rights, etc. But asking "why" is truly empowering. Until we ask the "why?" we actually become complicit in projects for which side effects, let alone intended effects, are not fully understood and, in fact, entirely underresearched because they were never questioned or researched under a holistic integral perspective.

Dane tells me, "I don't think we are dealing with sanity here on any level." He points out, "These are the same people that have detonated 1,800 nuclear bombs around the globe contaminating all life on earth to a degree," and adds, "I could only rationally think that those in power, knowing what we know about them already, would welcome a population that is not firing on all neurons, one that is not able to think so clearly and respond accordingly."

## Why We Are Still So Clueless

A professor and I were walking together, discussing a lecture we had both just attended. He then turned to me, looking deeply concerned, and out of the blue lowered his voice to blurt out that he and his colleague have discovered nanoparticles in the air that are extremely harmful. All I could really muster to comment with was, "Oh." He again confirmed to me that we are now breathing some extremely tiny, highly dangerous particles that are in the air. Wondering if there could be any link, I recalled that a few people I know have been struggling with respiratory problems for which doctors have no substantial insight. But although he was visibly concerned with what he had found, he only said further that he and his colleague will be continuing to study what is going on; we left it at that. I asked no questions because I hadn't grasped the enormity of what he was saying at the time. I was clueless.

I asked Dane why there is so little awareness over chemtrails. He recalls that recently he was told by a group of climate change scientists, "Unless or until geoengineering is acknowledged in one of their ordained publications, then it doesn't exist. It is not a reality." Dane explains that this is the mindset of much of academia right now and asserts, "As you know, publications are in one form or another supported by that power structure itself."

Certainly it is true that in all of academia, publications are supported and funded by specific groups of power holders within the hierarchy of power structures. There is a technical term in politics for this called "governmentality." It refers to the overt practices of government or the art of governing people who are hierarchically beneath the structure and therefore subject to a "power over" in which they can be directed to think and believe in particular ways. However, it is not just government—any entity with power has governing power over people's thinking and choice of actions. In fact, some are so powerful that government itself is a tool. But more significantly, with governmentality people govern themselves, meaning they adopt the mentality and essentially reward and punish themselves for being or not being in line with certain ways of conduct that become desirable in individuals' thinking.

The significance here is that the information we do not receive—as well as new terminologies to inform how to think—is part of the art of governing. Just as well, the denial of scientific information in journals of "good repute" is an art of governing. Dane adds that the scientists he has been contacted by at universities, such as, Stanford, Harvard, Duke, and UC Florida, confirm that trying to get this information out has been utterly frustrating. Of course, not just academic publications but universities themselves will be part of numerous techniques. Media is probably the most important tool. There are various tools of power that are involved in directing information, thought, and desire.

### Chemtrails and Action
Dane tells me,

> This is the last thing I wanted to believe was happening. I was very skeptical when I first heard about it. For about two years I was skeptical until I started doing my own testing. But once you do the math on how much material is falling on us and the fact that we are breathing it in, and the stats reflect that we have Alzheimer's, and autism stats from

two months ago [2013] that show a 10,000 percent increase in autism since 1975, one in fifty now has autism, one in three seniors in the continental US now dies with Alzheimer's or Dementia, not dies from it but with it, and once you look at the respiratory ailments, the respiratory mortality, and you have dozens of lab tests as we have, you know absolutely positively without any shadow of speculation that we are sucking this stuff in with every breath we take. I can't imagine any more immediate fight. Unless I can walk out and breathe, I mean the most basic human need, I can't turn away from this. I can't think of any greater priority than to walk outside and breathe without sucking in heavy metals.

There are a great many things affecting the climate. Human activity has many aspects to it, but the greatest single effect mathematically by shear scope and scale is certainly geoengineering. From the data we have, it is affecting everything from the entire web of life from the sky to the ground, from the atmosphere microbes, which studies show are possibly responsible for 80 percent of precipitation, photosynthesis; not only are 22 percent of the world's direct rays being blocked, but we have a shredded ozone which allows more of the harmful rays to penetrate through. And the light that does come through is an altered wavelength form and I know of no studies that address that effect on photosynthesis. We have a vitamin deficiency of some 98 to 99 percent of the population in California. The implications of being vitamin D deficient are quite horrific over the long term.

As these materials are coming down they appear to be sterilizing soils. As you eliminate the beneficial microbes, you have a host of non-beneficial organisms that take over. Just like the human body, without antibiotics the funguses take over. So, now, with the latest species' extinction rate based on the latest figures of as much as 200 species a day of plants and animals going extinct, 70–80 percent of that is fungal related.

It's time that people realize they have been part of a grand and lethal experiment that has decimated the planet's life support system and their health. Once they realize this, the game changes. Nobody is going to accept that. I hope that those people participating in the programs will realize that they are killing themselves, their own posterity, and their own people with them. I can only hope and pray that they refuse to participate at some point.

Dane acknowledges that various forms of human activity has enabled this dire situation; however, he argues that geoengineering is the greatest causal factor. He further argues that one cannot affect any part of the system without affecting all of the system. The interdependent effects, as observed in all disciplines of science and social science, are ignored. This singular linear approach to the neglect of all interconnected systems offers no solutions. Therefore, a higher consciousness of interconnecting parts is the only way to identify clear links and solutions. Dane illustrates how a wider view must be considered to move forward.

Although Dane had never envisioned struggling for awareness and action, he has dedicated his life to this cause for over ten years. And although he does not accept the label of "activist," the premise that he follows, as do all spiritual activists, is primarily one of purpose. Recognizing that he works with keys that enable success, I ask him to describe what keeps him going. He tells me, "The philosophy I operate with that keeps me going is that a person, I feel, should want to do the right thing because it is the right thing to do."

There is a pivotal aspect of embracing purpose that too many activists miss in whatever cause they take up. He identifies it, "Too many people won't take any action if they don't feel they are guaranteed a certain result. I hope people get away from that." Ironically this is the key that has enabled activists to truly succeed. It is not the focus of the goal no matter how serious it may be but, in fact, the process. He points out, "Everybody has a tremendous amount of power in this equation because of the Internet. People can find credible data. They can locate groups, organizations, and individuals that would care, if they had a clue, and they could send out these flaming arrows of credible data with the source for more data. And people will start to connect the dots because they know the weather is horribly off."

He provides California as example. In California, where he confirms quite a political spectrum exists, all sides are joining hands together on this issue because they know it is a common cause on which all depends. He explains, "If people stopped looking at how dark the horizon is and started to take action, I think that they would be much more energized and realize that they have tremendous power." I ask him what practical steps can be taken given the momentous challenges. He answers,

I will point out the mathematical equation. If one person passes on credible data to two people at the beginning of a thirty day month and raises awareness among those two people and those two people each tell two on the second day of the month, if that carries on for thirty days, that is 5.5 million people. People think my math is wrong on that. It is absolutely correct math. That is how exponential the equation can get if people simply started to take action instead of sitting.

Dane further explains, "You can't get through the system anymore. The system is bought, sold, paid for and in total lockdown." In dealing with governmentality, oftentimes one can only work from outside the system. He tells me that agencies from the U.S. Environmental Protection Agency (EPA), the California Energy Commission, Fish and Game, and Federal EPA have been set up to not reflect these programs, and describes,

So, we have to do it from the ground up. If people start spot fires by again waking up groups and organizations that once they know this is very lethal and a very immediate threat to them then those spot fires should burn on their own. And if we can start enough of these spot fires they all merge together so you can't ignore the fire anymore. And if we get this out in the open, truly in the open, I think at that point the game will change. I believe there are a lot of good people in our military that would realize what they are being a part of, not some benevolent planet saving program but quite the opposite. I think that's our best bet.

∾

# ⤟ 22 ⤞

# Compassionate Justice: A Just Third Way as Economic System

*"What else can we do? We do what we can do. If we can set good examples, then we're successful. Even if the whole civilization collapses, we've succeeded in showing future generations how to proceed."*

## Introduction

As Robert D. Crane describes to me, economic wealth drives politics. He raises a number of critical points while moving past the linear atomistic thinking of world economics in which, therefore, greed currently drives politics. He attempts thereby to expand this level of thinking in which power, might, and money are deciding factors rather than principles that offer a different economic system to the existing choices. He encapsulates these principles in an economic system called the Just Third Way and premises this system on his theory of compassionate justice. He suggests Qatar as a possible model in development of this Just Third Way but argues that the real success of our actions is setting an example in trying, even if a global shift does not occur in our civilization.

Robert Crane completed his Doctor of Laws (J.D.) at Harvard University, where he founded the *Harvard International Law Journal* and became the first president of the Harvard Law Society. Among numerous appointments, he served as Policy Advisor to Richard Nixon who appointed him as Deputy Director of the National Security Council. President Reagan appointed him as ambassador to the United Arab Emirates. He focuses on his passion for economic planning, as he has held several such consultancy roles for Middle Eastern states and particularly through his position on the board of directors and advisory council of the Center for Economic and Social Justice.

*Lessons in Economics and Compassion*

We can often recall situations in our lives that were pivotal for the directions and actions we chose afterward. Events help shape who we have become and how we choose to extend who we have become to the world. Crane recalls pivotal points in his life regarding a growing awareness of economics, learning compassion, discovering mental strength to endure and the concept of justice.

> Economics has gone through my entire life. My father taught economics at Harvard. I used to sit upstairs secretly listening to his conversations. He would invite his students occasionally and they would discuss the Great Depression. I had a very good education in the Depression. My father would teach summer school, so in the summer we would just get in the car and drive around the United States. And we saw the worst of the Depression. People just can't imagine it nowadays.

There was one day we were sitting in front of a motel. My grandmother was with us to get ready to go again. And this guy came along with his wife. She could hardly walk. He was carrying a baby and he said, 'Can you take my baby because we can't feed the baby.' My father asked, 'Why, what's the problem?' He said, 'Well, I work for a steel plant down in Texas but it closed. We put everything we could into a car and started driving up to Minnesota because I heard there were jobs in Minnesota. And our car caught on fire so everything burned up and now we're trying to hitch hike there. And nobody will pick us up. And we can't feed the baby and our last hope is, can you take our baby?'

My father said, 'Well, I can't but let's go over to that house over there and maybe they can.' So, we went over there and they took the baby, and said, 'Whenever you can get a job, let us know, and we'll take the baby up to you.' Then my father asked, 'What will you do if you can't get a job in Minnesota?' And then he said, 'Well, then I'll rob banks.' I was thinking, but you're not supposed to rob banks. But what else can they do? This is my introduction to economics.

Crane recalls that it was about that time that Roosevelt's New Deal was introduced into all these economic programs where there was no safety net in the beginning. He describes that back then people would actually starve. There was no minimum wage. He tells me, "I had a great uncle, the black sheep of the family, who would pay people ten cents an hour. It wasn't enough to survive on, but it was the only jobs that some people could get." This observation was also pivotal. He continues,

So, I thought, either you have Communism, which is just going to turn everybody into a serf—supposedly, they will be free and they'll own the government, where really there will be an elite radical group of Communists who will run everything. Or you have Capitalism, which is just going to concentrate wealth more and more. Karl Marx was right. Or you have something else. The Just Third Way is something President Reagan liked. He saw it as the only solution.

Crane gained a deep sense of compassion particularly through the example of his grandmother. He describes the experience.

The most important person in my life was my grandmother, my father's mother. My parents got a divorce because my father's family is Cherokee Indian and my mother's family was very wealthy and they considered him a barbarian. I was farmed off to my father's parents for a year. My grandmother was a very devout Christian. And she would walk around the house singing the hymns and reading the Bible an hour every day. I had no religious upbringing up until then and I was six years old, and this really influenced me.

She had a home not far from where she lived. It was a private house, and when I was there, there were six, sometimes ten, wayward women. They were women who had babies out of wedlock, and when that happened back then, they were pariahs. You had to put them in a home, and so she took care of these wayward girls. And for the rest of her life they would contact her and say to her, 'You were the most influential person in my life; I'm so happy you set me on the right path.' She was sort of my model of a human being. If I were to look at other people, there aren't really any models like that. She was. She taught me that the good thing about doing 'good' is to do 'good.' Rabia said, 'Oh Allah help me not to want to be a good person in order to go to heaven or to avoid hell but because You love me and I love You.' I don't worry about hell or heaven—whatever God wants I accept but I do care about doing what He created me to do. I have always thought there has got to be a purpose.

Crane's purpose was to provide a third way for an economic system, based on two essential pillars: compassion and justice. He wanted to learn more about justice. He tells me how he attempted it and in the process learned what success really is:

I was jailed by the Communists in 1948. I have always been interested in justice because as a kid I had seen a lot of injustice. So my father said if you want to study justice and injustice, go to Germany. Then I met some students there who had been in the underground against Hitler. I had escaped twice. I probably was the only person who has escaped twice from a Communist prison. But my experience in the prison was interesting because none of the people I had talked to had any idea why they were there and none of them expected ever to get out.

And they told me that nobody here can survive longer than two years because there is almost no food. Their immune system goes down and they die. I got out only because I pretended I was crazy. It taught me that some people grow stronger when they're in a hopeless situation. A person is free no matter where and no matter what conditions. You can be enslaved in a labor camp but you can still be free. No matter what the world gives you or whatever happens, you are still free to be yourself. Nobody can enslave the human soul and that is what I learned in the prison there. Because everyone else had given up and I had wondered, why had they given up? If people think I've failed in doing something, I don't care. I don't think I failed. I tried. That's success. Trying is success. If you stop trying, you fail.

*Today's Rules of Economics and the New Third Way*

Crane describes today's rules of economics and offers a new third way:

There are certain rules of economics. The first one is economics is binary, according to Karl Marx and according to everyone you will learn from in universities. Value consists of labor. Labor is the basic value of production. Machines, according to Karl Marx, are congealed labor. So, you want to get rid of the Capitalists. Laborers should govern and they should have their own government. Binary economics teaches that there are two factors to production, one is labor and the other is capital. And as we become more and more capital intensive, capital produces wealth much more than labor. Ten percent of the wealth in the world now is produced by labor. Ninety percent is by capital—ownership of machines, management systems, everything that has to do with producing wealth. One percent of the people in the world own the capital.

And another problem is that credit is given to those who are already rich in order to get money to invest, and most wealth comes from people who invest. They have enough wealth already to get credit to invest. Ninety-nine percent of the people do not have enough wealth to get credit to invest. So, the government creates money out of nothing. It doesn't cost something to create money. You give it to separate accounts called capital homestead accounts where every person in America, for example, from birth to death would get a certain amount every year on condition that they invested in productive investments, in real goods, and no consumption. Their consumption is going to come from their labor and then later from profits from their investments. It's calculated that by the time a person retires he should have an estate worth a million dollars and in the meantime he should be able, out of the profits—as he would be part owner of the trillions of dollars of future wealth—to pay his own education, his own health, except for extraordinary illness, his own retirement. Nobody would have to worry about retirement again because they would all own dividends. So, you would have a balance between input and output.

Now you have input by a lot of wealthy people and not enough people to buy it. If they owned capital themselves, you would have an enormous consumer's market and you would have input—output, contributive justice, both labor and capital, distributive justice, profits from both your labor and your capital. And then I invented a concept of harmonic justice.

There is a function for government. This government should make sure that there is a balance. The Libertarians don't like this idea because they don't like government to do anything. I say government has a function, but this function is just to make sure it doesn't have to do everything for people. This function is basically to work itself out of responsibility. President Reagan strongly advocated this and, as a matter of fact, I got six senators and six members of House of Representatives to introduce a bill to create a Presidential taskforce on economic justice, and Reagan was sort of the godfather of it. We produced two big books as a result of this. But it was so visionary that the Republicans absolutely freaked out. As a matter of fact, Reagan started talking about the Second American Revolution. We need a Second American Revolution. And I always say, no, we don't need a second one; we need to complete the first one. It is a way to promote justice and really the only way to counter global terrorism.

Crane argues that it is a response to injustice and warns, "If the wealth gap between countries keeps getting worse and worse, as it has been, global terrorism will become the global norm." His concern, however, includes a larger consequence. He continues, "And that will be the end of civilization." He comments that he is not sure that his approach will be possible, "And so automatically the richer get richer and the poorer get worse. This cannot continue without the destruction of civilization."

But he keeps going. With the Center for Economic and Social Justice, through which much of his activism takes place, he explains that when they have board meetings, the group has a litany of values and our goals, the last of which is, "You keep going, you keep going, you keep going." He explains, "If you aren't willing to do that then nothing else matters—you drop out."

To counter the existing system based on greed, as he calls it, the organization has a number of activities in which he is involved in promoting internationally. He explains, it has an equity expansion international, it does investment banking around the world in ways to invest ownership of a new corporation or an existing one in the workers, among many more. Its think tank works on addressing the institutions of society at the top. He adds, however, that its goals are embraced by a growing number of organizations around the world aiming to change the banking system.

## Who Will Lead a Just Third Way? Qatar

Crane tells me that institutions at the top are almost impermeable. He relays that some big capitalists agree with the Third Way approach but say it is not politically realistic. Also, he points out that the idea is too big— "People can't think that big." He tells me about many of the obstacles that such a program faces but adds, "You need vision." Talking to him from his office in Doha, he tells me, "And that's why I am here—because Sheikha

Mozah bint Nasser al Missned has the vision and I hope that she can carry it through."

He continues, "Her vision is to bring the best of all the religions and civilizations to Qatar in order to universalize the wisdom of them all and return it to the world in order to promote peace, prosperity, and freedom through transcendent and compassionate justice for everyone. She wants to return this to the world as the Islamic civilization did many hundreds of years ago. She thinks it can be done again. So do I."

Crane's approach, thus, is to include governments at the highest institutional levels as those who will lead the Just Third Way. He is, however, aware that there are obstacles. As he comments, "She's worried about the carbon based economy here declining, so she wants to develop manufacturing industries based, for example, on the rare metals in Afghanistan, supposedly 20 trillion dollars worth of wealth." But many countries have long known about an estimated 20 trillion dollars worth of resources in Afghanistan, first among them Germany who attempted negotiations with the Taliban.

He explains further his great worry,

> It's going to be China, India, Russia, the U.S. and they're all going to try to get a piece of that. I have dealt with the Taliban here . . . My concern is that it's going to be big multinational companies and there's going to be sovereign wealth funds. They're going to try to take all that wealth for themselves at the expense of everybody who lives there. This is the way it works.

He argues that every multinational corporation which wants to operate there should not own anything. Rather, the people who live there should own it, and corporations can have access that bring the profits back but with agreements. Given the monetary clout and vision, he says, "Qatar can do it. Nobody else would do it."

He believes Qatar can do it but only if the humanities are emphasized in its development. He argues, "Civilization consists of values. If you don't have values other than just power, those civilizations just die." On Qatar, he shares,

> If all we want to have is bigger and better petrochemical plants, Qatar will be a madhouse. It will be overthrown to begin with. Because there will be increasing concentration of wealth unless they adopt my system whereby everybody, every Qatari, would own these petrochemical resources. There would be no revolution. But only somebody like Sheikha Mozah can think this big and is not afraid to think this big.

### The Future of Civilization

Crane provides insight into the future. Although he continues to do what he feels is his purpose, his view provides us, I believe, a realistic prognosis if action for a Just Third Way is not embraced on a larger scale. He says, "I guess my experience in seeing the suffering in the earlier system influenced me and I see that this is going to get worse. Things are getting worse and they do at the end of every empire." He points out, "The Roman Empire, the Greek Empire—they all collapsed, and I think it's because first of all they lost the sense of building something beyond themselves, better than themselves, and then they saw some things kind of collapsing. Then they decided we have to survive at all costs. And that's the end of a civilization."

But his faith in the Divine is not only what keeps him going but it is also what provides him the right perspective. He confirms, "If we rely on ourselves to build a better world, we'll fail. If we rely on God, we have a chance. Otherwise, we have no chance." He does not rely on his own actions but gives over all worries to the Divine. In fact, he confirms, therefore, he does not worry. In view of the future, however, he explains, "I write all my books from the perspective of people 500 years from now who want to know, why did it go wrong and ask, 'How can we learn?'"

He beautifully concludes with his philosophy and perspective of the future:

> I am pessimistic about the future of the entire world and I am getting more and more pessimistic. On the other hand, that doesn't worry me. I don't think in terms of success. I think in terms of how can we set an example for people some time later when the situation is better. Models, I would like to build models. Qatar could be a large-scale model. All the problems that exist are here.
>
> What else can we do? We do what we can do. If we can set good examples, then we're successful. Even if the whole civilization collapses, we've succeeded in showing future generations how to proceed. Otherwise people there will say there's nothing you can do. I am optimistic but only within the framework

of God being the real decision-maker. If I would only trust human beings, I would have no hope. I would do nothing. I would go to the Riviera and do scuba diving or go up and train sled dogs in Alaska.

But I don't rely just on human beings although I have the philosophy of trusting individuals. My wife always tells me that I am too trusting of people and am usually wrong. I always tell her that she is not trusting of individuals and usually right, but I trust people. It makes me happier.

∼

# Conclusion

These spiritual activists are people like you and me. There is nothing special about them that enabled them to choose to create a different and better life than any of us. But each of them are changing the world. We all have our own unique and special calling to contribute our part. This is the key. Only you can know what your deepest desire is. You likely have many promptings. You can access this knowing. Ultimately your path to finding meaning and fulfillment rests in you.

The way forward for all of us is to remind ourselves of the keys to this ultimate success and remind ourselves that we have the Source and power to transform our lives and contribute to change in the world. Yes, each of us. Finding purpose and learning how to flow with universal wisdom to extend your highest expression can be easy if you use the right keys, align with your principles, and discern appropriate strategies. This book is an invitation for you to practice using and embodying these keys, principles and strategies. I wish you joy, peace, and light. May you always stand firm in your core of who you really are and express it. The world is waiting.

More information, intensive courses and further support can be found at *spiritualactivismonline.com*.

# About the Author

 Wanda Krause grew up in the north of Canada in Whitehorse, Yukon. She then travelled extensively and completed a PhD in politics, at the University of Exeter in the United Kingdom. She also studied spirituality and integral thinking. During her extensive travels, she has participated alongside many of the activists she has studied. She strives to meld the two paths of politics and spiritual practice in hopes of bringing consciousness and enthusiasm to activism.

She currently teaches in public policy on planning and strategic management and was previously founding coordinator of a master's program in Qatar; senior lecturer at the Department of Politics and International Studies, SOAS, University of London; and research fellow at the London School of Economics (LSE), UK. Wanda is the author of *Women in Civil Society*, New York: Palgrave-Macmillan; and *Civil Society and Women Activists in the Middle East*, London: I.B. Tauris. She is also a *Kosmos* journal ambassador.

# Notes

1   Alana Semuels."Wages of Top 1% Rise Much Faster than Bottom 90%." *Los Angeles Times*, October 19, 2011, http://latimesblogs. latimes.com/money_co/2011/10/wages-of-top-1-rise-much-faster-than-bottom-90.html

2   William L. Simon and Jeffrey S. Young. *iCon: Steve Jobs, The Greatest Second Act in the History of Business*. Hoboken, New Jersey: John Wiley & Sons, 2005

3   Walter Isaacson. *Steve Jobs*. New York: Simon & Schuster, 2011.

4   Marianne Williamson. *Everyday Grace: Having Hope, Finding Forgiveness, and Making Miracles*. New York: Riverhead Books, 2002.

5   Danah Zohar and Ian Marshall. *Spiritual Intelligence: The Ultimate Intelligence*. New York: Bloomsbury, 2001.

6   Cindy Wigglesworth. *SQ 21: The Twenty-One Skills of Spiritual Intelligence*. New York: Select Books, 2012.

7   Ibid., 8.

8   Ibid., 13.

9   Ervin Laszlo and Jude Currivan. *Cosmos: A Co-creator's Guide to the Whole-World*. New York: Hay House, 2008.

10  Ibid., 17.

11  Ibid., 67.

12  Ibid., 69.

13  'God' will be referred to in the masculine for simplicity throughout although God is unlike any creation and Divinely neither female or male but inclusive of masculine and feminine.

14  Marianne Williamson. *Illuminati: A Return to Prayer*. NewYork: Penguin Putnam, 1995.

15  Roger Cohen. "Report on Bosnia Blames Serbs for 90% of the War Crimes." *The New York Times*, March 9, 1995.

16  Ewa Tabeau and Jakub Bijak. "War-related Deaths in the 1992-1995 Armed Conflicts in Bosnia and Herzegovina: A Critique of Previous Estimates and Recent Results," *European Journal of Population*, Vol. 21, Issue 2-3. (2005)187-215.

17  Dan Bilefsky. "Karadzic Sent to Hague for Trial Despite Violent Protest by Loyalists," *The New York Times*, July 30, 2008. http://www.nytimes.com/2008/07/30/world/europe/30serbia.html?_r=0